Learning Through Encounter

Given

by the

Lincoln Christian College

Alumni Association

As Part

of a

$100,000 Gift,

1968-1971

Learning Through Encounter

Robert Arthur Dow

JUDSON PRESS, Valley Forge

LEARNING THROUGH ENCOUNTER

To my wife, Eleanor, and my children, Linda, Richard, Robert, and Russell, with whom to live is an exciting, everyday learning experience.

PREFACE

Changin', times are changin'
Some people think it's a doggone shame.
That nothin' but God
Is quite the same.[1]

It's hard to know much these days about anyone's credibility. Even God takes his knocks. It seems that everything, everyone, is coming unglued. The traditional images, forms, and symbols have little to say to today's world. Even churchmen are apologetic for using the words "God," "Jesus Christ," and "sin" outside the sanctuary. We are hard put to find any similes that can tell it like it is from one generation to another. In Jesus' day every word — mustard seed, sower, pearl, lamb — carried for generations a sense of reality common to an agrarian people who had settled down in one place and time, in a world they knew would remain the same for a while.

But we live in a time when we must not only accept changed conditions but also adjust to change itself. What terms can we use now that youth will comprehend in their adult years? Everything is fluid, like a river of water rushing from its source to its mouth. One place is never the same the moment after the moment before. The surface runs more swiftly than the deep, but the slow running deep changes the earthly contour permanently. The surface waters whisk away all (and only) the loose, the trivia. The deep current carries even the strongest institutions downstream. Everything is change.

What forms have we known to which we can cling for security? Not many! And now they are being challenged, too!

How relevant is the Christian faith to this changing world? Wherein lies the Christian faith's credibility?

[1] Sister Miriam Therese Winter, "Changin'" (New York: The Vanguard Press, 1968). Copyright by Medical Mission Sisters, 1968.

The Christian faith is more relevant now than ever before. In every age there have been critical moments when everything that seemed fixed came unglued. And it seems that in every age God has made the same claim. We ask:

To what form or structure are you committed?

How many offerings have you made in penance?

But the real questions still are:

Do you do justice?

Do you love kindness?

Do you walk humbly with your God? (Cf. Micah 6:8.)

How? This way, said Jesus! "Come — follow me!"

The question is not one of form, formula, or fame. It has been and always will be a question of relationship. God *is* relationship. But the relationship is composed of two very real parts: It is sameness and it is never the same. It is "the same, yesterday, today, and forever," and it is "forever changing." This is the paradox of God. He is a God who is always what he is; and yet he is forever the God of movement and of change. Even in change, there is a sameness; like the river that is always the same, and yet always different. Can we live with this kind of paradox?

Can mankind, so dependent upon keeping some things forever locked into a known form, learn to survive in this kind of reality? How much change can a man take? Is there support for him in the questionable seasons of his own change?

Immediately, two very biblical images come to the fore: first, the pilgrim; and second, the community.

This book tries to address these two essentials of the human journey: (1) man — the pilgrim, and (2) man — in community. The book is therefore an elemental synthesis of four disciplines: applied behavioral science, social psychology, experiential education, and Christian theology.

In preaching "process as mission" am I doing violence to our Christian heritage? I do not believe so. We have always preached program as mission! We must train men even more surely to be pilgrims living in a temporary, but vital, colony of heaven in an age that demands better performance and immediate satisfaction.

The hardest reality for me to accept is that even as I write, with long months until publication, what I project as a viable form for a day of change will more than likely have a challenger before the book is marketed. Today, to write is to risk.

What are the risks that go beyond the pen?

My greatest risk is simply to move wood from one pile to another without adding much to the fire of enlightenment. On the other hand, I could simply let the wood remain, *status quo*, without doing much of anything, except stomach the sterility of irrelevant form and tradition. My hope is to enlighten, while at the same time to encourage movement to the here-and-now concern for relevance and meaning; to meet the world head-on in encounter; to risk self-exposure and even ridicule.

To the progressive — the world has "outgrown God."

To the traditionalist — new disciplines are "demonic," a threat to what seems to be stable.

I perceive both approaches to be idyllic and defensive. On the one hand, the progressive presumes to live by works, while, indeed, he cannot live without faith. On the other hand, the traditionalist presumes to live by faith, while, indeed, he cannot without works. Life is both works and faith, role and person, routine and extraordinary, flat and dimensional.

Whatever disciplines are to be projected that will be helpful in learning, they must include both realms and permit the meeting, even the influencing, of one another. This joining of forces will permit a growing sense of mutuality with God, a partnership that will carry us beyond our adolescent insistence for rugged individualism to an adult posture of responsible action and reflection. The end product of this educational process will be to strengthen the individual who concerns himself with intervention on behalf of the poor and the oppressed, and fights against war, pollution, and discrimination.

This book presents a process for sharing in that responsibility. It presents the process in the context of the Christian faith. Our faith is not a religion, not a rite, not a form; it is A WAY. It *is* a process. The media, then, becomes the message. The message *is* the medium.

Why do we struggle so with this concept? Why do we say that it is new? John said it, only in different words: "And the Word became flesh and dwelt among us, full of grace and truth; we have beheld his glory, glory as of the only Son from the Father" (John 1:14).

As in Jesus' day, the response to the "word" in our own day will be diffuse. There will be some who will see this process as *the answer*. There will be others who will see this process as *a curse.* For me, this process lies between *the answer* and *a curse.* Process is a tool. Like any other tool, it is, in itself, neutral. In the hands of a dedicated educator, it can challenge the best of minds. It can revitalize and renew. It can redeem. In the hands of an anarchist, process can be vicious. It can tear down. Even at best, it will never meet the needs, the expectations, and/or the wants of everyone. No tool ever does.

I am writing for those who are "in between." The whole discipline of applied behavioral science addresses itself to those who are in between, always regarding matters of relationship and movement. This discipline permits the pilgrim the license to address change while it gives him a base of operation in community. What many of the applied behavioral sciences lack is a biblical and theological rationale, a framework that will enable them to see the relevance of this tool to the church's mission. Without this, because of rumor, periodic "bad" experiences, sensational journalism, and other less desirable factors, churchmen may reject a tool which could serve them well. (This kind of misunderstanding provoked a similar resistance to the Freudian system, which, after long delays, now strengthens our church's ministry.)

This book is an initial effort to answer the question, What is the biblical, theological, and educational basis for utilizing the applied behavioral sciences in the contemporary church? The book is written in three parts: *The Rationale, The Human Relations Skill and Theory,* and *The Application in a Church Setting.*

As I write this text, I am aware of the fact that there are many persons to whom thanks need to be expressed. Whatever may be the form and whatever may be the error, that I accept as my responsibility. But the motivation and content comes from the many who have taken a significant role in my life, especially in the last ten years. It is difficult to know just who affected me the most and when. Broad reading in the field has served as "fill" which is cemented together by the experienced events occurring all over our country. My gratitude, then, must be general, except for my teacher and mentor Dr. John Vayhinger, my senior trainer Dr. Arnold Nakajima, and my colleague Mrs. Nancy Geyer. These three have given me special encouragement and specific training. Other contributors to this book are numerous and often anonymous. I wish to thank Lewis Johnson, Nate Turner, and Bob Sherbondy for their personal encouragement and advice. To the latter I am deeply indebted for his editorial comment and insight. He made me work harder to develop a more satisfying manuscript.

My special thanks are addressed to three earlier influences, my parents Mr. and Mrs. Henry B. Dow and Mrs. Luella Bridgeman, my fifth and sixth grade teacher. All three gave me experiences and learnings that have become the ground of all my understanding in experiential education. My gratitude also goes to my secretary, Mrs. Anne Shawver, who has labored long and hard on several manuscripts, as we have neared completion of this project.

BOB DOW

CONTENTS

PART I
The Rationale

1. PERSONAL PERSISTENT LIFE ISSUES

Where does one begin except in the here and now with man's personal persistent life issues? My objective is to increase the reader's knowledge and understanding of the rationale, the theory, and the application of the applied behavioral sciences in our church community life and mission enterprise. The implied style of this ministry suggests an ACTION-RESEARCH model. We act and learn as we face life together. Some educators call such a model a living and learning style. This style begins where we are, with who we are, and with what we are. The important concern is not who, what, or where — but that we begin. Whatever reflection or evaluation is done (and it must be done) must be done while in motion.

At one time we could carefully plan, act, and evaluate. But the age of the computer has changed all that. With change occurring at increasing speeds, it is impossible to comprehend what has happened before the happening is past and is moving on to the next event. Man is challenged just to keep up. Whatever learning is accomplished, and whatever transfer of learning is possible, must be done "on the spot." Whatever planning is done, is done "on the move."

This new mode of learning is terribly theatening to the individual. His needs for PERSONAL SECURITY and CREATIVE ADVENTURE collide continually. This conflict creates tension. As the tension mounts, the alternatives appear more ominous. How can I cope with my fear of the personal on the one hand and my need to be personal on the other hand? Such passion frightens even the most capable. The alternative? Neutralize! Cop out!

The most viable alternative to tension is neutrality, a form of legitimized escape. There are many forms of escape, of course, but only a few that are socially acceptable options for an individual to take; for example:

SOCIALLY UNACCEPTABLE	SOCIALLY ACCEPTABLE
Alcoholism	Religious fanaticism
Drug addiction	Financial success
Sexual promiscuity	Job commitment
Stealing	Compulsive action
Addiction to gambling	Social achievement
Murder	Material wealth
Psychotic behavior	Showmanship

If we agree that not all religious fanatics or Wall Street successes are escapists, how, then, can we judge the escapist as opposed to the realist?

The man who seeks neutrality is one who generally develops that part of the self which is proficiently professional AT THE EXPENSE OF HIS PERSONAL RELATIONSHIPS. This behavior is known as functionalism. He puts on "the mask," *persona.* (The *persona* denotes the mask worn by the Greek actor who, when he wanted to change character roles, simply exchanged one mask for another.)

The functionalist is one who is pragmatically involved in the business of: (a) survival of self, and (b) the seeking of self-approval. He has spent considerable time in life building a sense of achievement and success from which he gains some acknowledged acclaim from others, but severely criticizes himself as "not being good enough." This is the *persona,* the mask. "This is the 'role' that I want people to see — for it is easier to master that one facet of life than all," the functionalist rationalizes.

The first area of his life which suffers is the immediate personal area. The man has married because it is the thing to do; the relationship serves a functional role (sex and housekeeping). Children result from the union — but they need only financing; the wife (or some other social agent) can raise them. Soon, disillusioned, one of three situations results:

1. Separation through divorce
2. Separation through diversion of loyalties (no communication, though they *appear* to be married and function as a marriage)
3. Conflict, leading to change in the behavior of both persons, that develops into a mutual consummation of the marriage

The latter course of action is painful, and generally less apt to be taken than the first two. The reason? We tend not to want to deal with conflict. It is too painful. We prefer to avoid it.

Rest assured, persons who enjoy pain are sick (i.e. masochists, sadists, etc.). But persons who fail to heed pain, or learn from it, are persons who waste one of life's most important treasures. Pain means trouble. It is a warning that we ought to heed. Like tension, it is ground for creative action. If we are neutral-functional, we prefer to ignore ("it will go away on its own!"), eliminate ("you need surgery"), subjugate ("you need a tranquilizer"), compromise ("I'll give a little"), or just rationalize the conflict, hoping it will dissolve — not resolve.

DIAGRAM A

As Diagram A suggests, we all live in tension between two levels of experience: pain and pleasure. As line 1 indicates, we attempt to find some way of gaining immediate release when we are hurt. We assume that the nearest crutch is our means to pleasure. But when the effort is finished, as line 2 indicates, we find ourselves right back where we started. The next time (line 3), it will take more effort to escape than it did the first time (line 1). Lines 1, 3, and 5 represent the escape option: hyperactive worker, alcoholism, or any other addictive behavior. The goal: dissolve or avoid the pain.

The alternative at first appears painful. I say "at first" because generally it leads to ultimate relief and resolve. We begin as we did in Diagram A, with an awareness of pain. We attempt to find temporary release (line 1) but find that the resolve is little and only temporary. We seek help from a doctor, a counselor, a teacher, a friend, depending on what it is that is bothering us. If the help is productive, the pain level will more than likely increase (Diagram B, line 3) until the source of the hurt is revealed (S). Then the pain level diminishes as the causal factor is eliminated. It may subside in stages (4, 5, 6, 7) but it diminishes sufficiently so as to control the pain permanently and lend itself to creative growth.

Few elect to permit the latter process (Diagram B) to occur. They have too little confidence in their own ability to cope. Their largest level of potential remains untried, and, therefore, unknown. With support, we can stand much more pain than we realize. As psychologists report, we use only about 10 percent of our capabilities at any one time.

We are so filled with anxiety and fear of being afraid that we seek the alternative — neutrality (3, in Diagram C).

DIAGRAM B

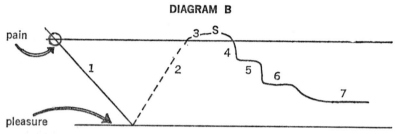

We have become a generation of Linuses. Dozens watch while a young woman is raped in an office building in New York; thirty or more see a woman murdered in the streets of a city; fifty watch a boy burn after a fall on a railroad track; neighbors watch an incensed man murder a young mother, his estranged wife; and do nothing. Why? In our efforts to hide our own ineptness, we plead "boredom," "you don't turn me on," "scapegoating," and a dozen other pleadings, as if motivating us is someone else's task. This behavior is projection.

Projection basically means that we load onto another our own unwanted feelings. Generally, this means keeping the desirable feelings and dumping the undesirable feelings on another.

To cope with this situation is to find help that will force each one to face his own feelings; to mirror them back. (I am not suggesting analysis here; I am suggesting rather, that in any good, healthy, adult relationship, persons own up to their feelings and, with sympathy, enable others to do the same.)

When I enter my home and find another person angry, why do I need to get angry (unless I am already angry)? What the other person needs is help in coping with his (her) feelings. If I reciprocate with hostility (my defense), then all is lost. But if I can say, "You are angry. What made you angry? Tell me." Then there is a chance for resolve, and, consequently, reconciliation.

DIAGRAM C

Life/Learning

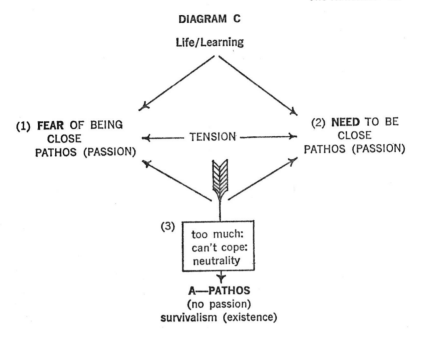

(1) FEAR OF BEING
CLOSE
PATHOS (PASSION)

←——— TENSION ———→

(2) NEED TO BE
CLOSE
PATHOS (PASSION)

(3) too much:
can't cope:
neutrality

A—PATHOS
(no passion)
survivalism (existence)

This course of action may, for a few moments, increase the pain level. But it will lead to permanent resolve rather than temporary appeasement and/or repression.

Tension, then, cannot be eliminated by a temporary neutralizing of the situation. It is a constant "ghost" of what could be if we trusted enough to risk facing the pain.

Taking no risk means (1) a low personal trust level, and (2) no possibility for real personal movement. We hear one say, "That's all right! I don't care, anyway!" But that, too, is a lie. Our defenses are too much with us.

What happens to us when we choose to be neutral is tragic. Like an old car left in neutral, we can be pushed and pulled everywhere, anywhere, by someone else's will. Where we go, how we get there, and when, is all clearly up to someone else. We have no power of our own. We've abdicated all responsibility. What we believe to be "our control" is not our control at all. It makes us even more controlled by others.

For example, John has trouble trying to resolve the conflicting demands which are placed upon him by his mother and his wife.

The demands are seriously in conflict. He deals with the tension by avoidance. He works fourteen hours a day, six days a week. He spends Sunday "working" at the church with the young people (a socially acceptable escape). This, John hopes, will control the situation and keep him safe. However, two very real factors become obvious:

1. The two women continue to haunt him in hope of winning his attentions, so he must continue to avoid them.
2. He is not free to choose what he wants to do with his life and time, since he must spend his energy running away.

He is trapped by his fear of hurting his mother or his wife by bringing into the open their conflicting demands.

Can we really help others by doing their thing *for* them? Or by protecting them? Help comes through community — doing things *with* them; feeling *with* them. What either woman is legitimately saying is: "I'm afraid that if I am honest with him, he may turn on me and hurt me back." This reaction is a prejudicial act motivated by the will to protect oneself from what one anticipates as the real hurt.

In the long run, we tend to hurt more by avoiding the conflict. We are in more danger when we fail to address the beloved with our feelings than when we do. Openness, the truth "spoken in love," begets openness, as trust begets trust. For a time, there may be some increase of the pain level, but the ultimate resolve is more permanent. The only real control is trust. Anything short of this is temporary and shoddy.

Let's make this process of finding resolve concrete. The Council of the East Oakland Baptist Church has been meeting for almost a year. Gene has been serving as chairman while the others have assumed various roles as leaders in church committee work. At the September meeting the council had two items on the agenda: (1) decide upon the budget for the next year; and (2) resolve the conflict over alternative proposals for church action: (a) relocate or renovate the present facilities, (b) defer building plans for the church and allocate $30,000 for a low income housing project, or (c) hold the line for another few years.

But at that particular meeting the group met a stalemate in trying to choose among the alternative proposals for action. Therefore, they could only propose a budget based upon the spending of the last year. Carl, Glen, and Bill were very much in favor of relocating and selling the present church to a black community group. Mary Lou, Randall, and George had worked for months getting the housing project proposal ready. They needed $30,000 just to get underway. Ralph, representing the older, more conservative members, was angry. He felt that the people could not meet a new financial challenge or support any of the urban programs that made it easy for those "lazy poor" and "vicious blacks." Wendell was on the fence, but tended to be swayed by Ralph.

All of the arguments in the meeting ended in accusations. Everything was subjective and strained. Finally, Ralph walked out of the meeting. Gene came away from the September meeting feeling frustrated and desperate, asking himself, "Is this really what the church is all about? Why am I involved?"

The Christian education director had planned a weekend laboratory in early October for training church committee leadership. Gene invited Carl, Mary Lou, and George from the council to attend with him, and they consented. In all, twenty-two persons attended.

On Friday evening, they worked on factors relating to verbal and nonverbal communication. On Saturday, they worked together in teams at problem-solving and decision-making models. Communications were improved as the day went on. In the Saturday evening session the teams spent time defining the real issues they faced in the church situation. The council members discovered that they had really set a self-defeating course. They had made their assumptions, not on the basis of facts, but on the subjective level of personal interest and involvement. By late Sunday afternoon, they had enough insight and steam to move into the October meeting with renewed hope. They called Ralph and encouraged him to return to the council.

As the October meeting got underway, Gene showed both anxiety and excitement. He was hopeful. Ralph was the last to come. The team seemed relieved when he arrived. Gene opened with prayer: "Lord, we've got a lot to do — for the church needs to move. Help us to do only that which will reflect the spirit of love and commitment. Help us, O God, to be what we want the church to be — here and now."

His voice showed his anxiety. The board members fell silent, apprehensive. They had come to the meeting ready for a fight. Again, the way they sat indicated the "side" they had already taken. The pastor was somewhat withdrawn from the circle, indicating his own fearsome position.

George was the first to speak. "You know, I've thought a lot about what happened here last month in our meeting. We were certainly a living contradiction. *(Pause.)* I mean, I didn't show much consideration for any of you others. I really didn't listen to your words, your hopes, your fears, especially to the considerations that Ralph expressed. I'm sorry he left. But I can understand why he did. But I was also wondering why I was so all-fired-sure that my position was the best! I've always felt that I had the best interest of the church at heart. But, in thinking it over, I guess there are some other things happening to me, too." There was a long pause. Then George went on.

"I've been wanting to beat out Glen *(he looked across the table squarely at Glen)* ever since he pulled that deal with John Mc-Carthy. I told him then that I thought it was a rotten deal. I felt that I had proven myself to be right. We ended up paying a whole lot more for that boiler than it was worth. Ever since then, I've wanted to say, 'There, I told you so!' But I never had the chance, until now, I guess. And I'm ashamed.

"Then there's that study group on the housing project that I represent. I've made some strong personal ties in that study group. We really believe in what we are doing. And I don't want to let them down. They're depending upon me to get the money for the housing project program. But I know that the total church has some reservations about our becoming slum landlords and a community settlement house operator. We haven't tried to involve the whole church in the planning because we felt it would create too much open conflict." He ended by saying, "I think I've been wrong about this. Not the project we proposed, but in the reasons for pushing it the way I have. I wonder how you others feel about it?"

This was just the beginning. The pastor listened to the interchange with both excitement and anxiety. *I wonder what will happen if they all start to unload?* At one point, he attempted to cut it off. *After all,* he thought, *the housing project is my pet project, too. I don't want to rock the boat right now. And there is the task of making the "right" decision to present to the church body next week. This might end up being an all-night session and we still may have no decision. Can we really risk this?*

But as the council members talked, a new atmosphere began to develop. When it became uncomfortable, Gene added some light-hearted banter while George kept the focus on the matters at hand. There were significant references to the "mission of the church," "the meaning of reconciliation," and the "gospel of concern." Mary Lou talked about the decision-making experiences they had in the weekend human relations laboratory.

Finally, Mary Lou suggested that they all stand in a circle and link elbows together. "Now," she announced, "to yourself, concentrate on one spot in this room. Get that spot firmly fixed in your mind." There was a pause. "Now, without saying a word, take the whole group to that spot." There were a few objections. Someone asked, "What's this got to do with our problem?" "You'll see! Try it!" Mary Lou answered. Action!

It was all over in less than three minutes. There was no need for further explanation. The concrete action spoke loudly. The council members sat around the table and reflected on the experience. "I see it now," one member shared. "We all have our own ideas about how things should really go. Unless we give each one a chance at his own thing, we may never reach any of our goals together." There were echoes of reinforcement.

"True," Mary Lou responded. "And, furthermore, if I can't influence you, I'm sure you are not going to influence me either."

Gene broke into the discussion with a brief spontaneous prayer. There were tears in his eyes. For the first time in his life, the council, bent upon a task, had become a living, breathing church.

They clasped hands around the table and felt a fellowship that they had never experienced before. They prayed. They were ready to at least try a new way of working together. They decided that all their plans would be held in abeyance until the congregation could be informed about every move that was being considered. The church began a whole new program of strategic planning (see chapter 12).

This episode can be duplicated over and over. Boards, committees, classes, family groups, all find this experiential process meaningful. Now, every situation has the potential for a happening and for learning.

What happened?

Three different points of view were developed by three separate groups of people, each group working with a different set of assumptions, a different reservoir of data, with a subjective perception that limited their view of the whole. With heads down, seeing only their own thing, they found it impossible to keep the whole church in view. Any attack forced a polarization. Each person's defenses came up. The battle lines were drawn. The win/lose war was on.

All the talking was wasted, being deflected by the defenses of the "enemy." The "enemy" either had to go around the defense and strike a deadly blow (which happens sometimes), or simply pound away at the defenses until the other "enemy" goes away or crumbles under the opposing force. The object of this game is *to win.*

In this kind of encounter, no one ever gives in willingly because that means being wiped out, taken over, or beaten.

The proper intervention can assist those involved to perceive their behavior for what it is, and lead to a learning that can enable the participants to change their objective from the need to win agreement to the desire to be understood. Then each stands ready to be influenced by the other. There is movement toward mutual understanding which is the ground of all consensus decision making.

What do we mean by the phrase "the proper intervention"? This may well be an encounter that copes more directly with the blocking factors than with the motivating strengths. It may mean that we deal first with the fears that keep us defensive.

Our tendency is to try to talk persons out of their defenses without dealing with the fears that lead to their defensiveness. This is not possible except through a manipulation of the worst sort.

To understand is to be aware of what is happening, to whom, and why. To understand is to be grounded in the kind of self-knowledge that builds empathy. And empathy is the ground of love that leads to a mutual sense of trust. The alternative is only a desperate neutrality.

Let us summarize. What has been suggested here are basically guidelines for developing any personal persistent life issue encounter. Briefly stated, they include:

1. *Interact here and now.* Deal with the issue as it is; do not exclude the influence of the past nor a vision of the future; but be fully aware of the fact that the NOW is where the action is. Be relevant.

2. *Trust enough to take some risks.* To hold on to security at the expense of the need for creative adventure is to die without bringing into actuality your fullest potential. Do not take care-

less and unconsidered risks, but do strive to enlarge a personal pilgrim faith that can find support in a genuine community of concerned persons.

3. *Assume responsibility for yourself, your feelings, and behavior.* Scapegoating, sniveling, and dramatic martyrdom are neurotic complexes that bring only further hurt and the need for more arduous acts of escape. Make a more conscious effort to control not others, but yourself, in every situation. Be open, ready to respond, and free to receive as well as give.

4. *Face into the conflict in the hope of resolve.* To hope for a conflict to dissolve is to play the "dreamer's game." Moreover, it is to miss a creative opportunity for growth.

5. *Seek not to win agreement, but to achieve understanding.* With at least one person in every encounter willing for this to happen, there is a possibility that goes beyond all the expectations of the world. For this is God's way, as revealed in Jesus Christ. In him there was no will to either win or curse. He willed only to love and redeem. That gospel remains relevant in our day.

6. *Respect another's defenses. Love him.* Every man has his defenses. The defenses define the man. Defenses lend themselves to what otherwise might end in chaos. They stabilize a person's life. What cannot happen by force, love can make happen because it does not insist on its own way. Ready to endure even as it persists, love may be invited in where otherwise fear has controlled.

2. EXPERIENTIAL EDUCATION: A PROCESS PHILOSOPHY OF EDUCATION

There is never a time in our lives when we do not learn. Therefore, it is to the advantage of educators to encourage the most creative and productive kind of learning. This is experiential education at its best. In an age that is modified by words such as "rapid," "changing," "tremendous," "mobile," "expansive," "over-productive," any educational forces must be both behavioral and process oriented; behavioral because of the decreased time lapse between learning and application and process oriented because the increase in motion demands on-the-spot action-reflection and change. Life is a matter of seeking a meaningful essence effective while in change. It is no longer a matter of joining up with the "right" institution in the hope of fixed security.

The principal argument for experiential education is that learning is only learning when new behavior results from the process. On the other hand, conceptual development is a "learning about" something, not learning in and of itself.

The experiential philosophy of education grows out of a basic question: How *do* people learn? An answer to that question must assume, I believe, five factors as criteria for verification of a useful philosophy of education.

1. *The learning must be current.* Many disciplines are struggling against obsolescence. New trends force us to consider new ways of coping with each new crisis. To refashion the old, to retrieve the valued, and to grasp the vital among the innovative is the business of experiential education. We must weigh both old and new, and, through a selective process, create a meaningful synthesis that is relative to the here and now, in the full knowledge that this movement, too, will pass.

2. *The learning must be eclectic.* For years, men of various philosophical persuasions claimed that they had found the new heaven and the new earth. They jealously guarded their findings,

giving glimpses of their newfound truth to only a selected few who were separated from the human race to be entrusted with this new truth. Men within their own disciplines threatened the existence of others, who, like themselves, were in pursuit of some theological, psychological, or political truth. Each felt that he held the one single truth that would save all mankind.

No one discipline, no one system, holds *the* truth for all time and for all men. The whole question about life has not yet been asked. How, then, can there be a whole answer before there is a whole question? Experiential education is a process available to every sphere of exploration and discovery. This process challenges its users to test the validity of their own assumptions.

3. *The learning must be inclusive.* It follows from the above that all that is known must contribute to the ongoing search for new knowledge. No one discipline or school of thought has an edge on wisdom and truth.

4. *The learning must deal with the essentials, not structures and forms.* This fact appears obvious in our day of change. But for years, we have tooled our leadership to deal with structures and forms, trivia and dogma. They have carried this excess baggage (ready-made programs) from community to community, from church to church, from event to event, feeling that it was imperative that every phase be completed faithfully. This format might have been viable in the past, but today most of it is excess. Men living in a space age travel with only the barest of essentials. They must be ready to develop on-the-spot data for their analysis, planning, action, and evaluation. The action is the focus, while reflection, in a subservient position, must lead the actors to a better expenditure of time, money, and life. This kind of here-and-now skill requires careful training and a high level of personal discipline.

5. *Learning must be dynamic.* Many of us resist facing conditions that utilize the emergent design process. We prefer careful planning and controls. We plead for time: time to think; time to write it out; time to plan; time to evaluate. This kind of time is not available. All of us are students — all of the time. All of us, then, must be teachers — all of the time. Our concern for the dynamic does not eliminate our concern for content. We must be aware that the very content is shaped by the dynamic: the medium must reflect the message. The medium *is* the message. Learning in the experiential sense must be alive and free to grow whenever it is found.

In summary, experiential education addresses behavior, not attitude; it deals with action, not concepts. It is a process philosophy. Its principal thesis is that learning is only learning when it results in some new behavior.

Experiential education is current, eclectic, inclusive, essential, and dynamic. It takes into account the serious question: HOW DO PEOPLE LEARN?

People learn *from experience*. (The truth is that too few people learn from their experiences.) Most people get caught up in the pressures of life's continuous demand: survive — produce — achieve. They move quickly from one action (activity) to another. There is no time for deliberate reflection, learning, or appreciation (the essence of worship). Our activist colleagues insist on making even our Sunday morning "worship" event another experience, often over-programmed with prayers, music, readings, and speeches.

Developing an experience into a living-learning situation requires a disciplined and conscious effort on the part of the learner to *stop* the action and return to it, asking: "What happened?"

Can I identify things that happened in this experience, remaining descriptive and specific? To whom did it happen, and how? When did it happen? What preceded it? What followed? Can my observations be specific, reality oriented, tested out? Can I avoid hypothesizing ("If you had done it. . . .") and really face the facts ("When you said. . . .")?

What was really happening? Can I analyze the experience in such a way as to be able to see what made things happen the way they did? What seemed to be the behavior that was the most helpful? What or who blocked the process? What really hindered things from moving on, developing further? Who was being responsible, irresponsible? Were the results satisfying or disappointing?

What can we learn that is applicable in other situations? Can I generalize from this specific event so that the next time I face a similar event, I can be more appropriate in my responses, more helpful in my action? What are my learnings specifically? Am I willing to work at transferring these new learnings into my general living through deliberate practice and application? This process can be, and often is, painful. It requires the unlearning of other behaviors less conducive to our personal development and the acquisition of the new. It is often easier to yield to the old patterns to which we have grown accustomed than to change.

This yielding heightens the tragedy of our lives. As psychologists have indicated, we are ruled by the developments of our early childhood experiences, especially those initial emotional encounters in the first six years (some say the first three years) of our lives. Our fantasy years that lead to puberty and adolescence serve only to reinforce our childhood life-learnings.

The tragedy is that we commit the weightier adult years of our lives to the subservience of our infantile experiences — an unmanageable past. Thus self-knowledge is important to facilitate understanding. Experiential education, though it is more than self-knowledge, frees the learner to reduce the controls of the past and redesign his life in light of a more manageable future. *To make a conscious use of the self is the essence of a constructive life.* In order to accomplish this task each learner must have the tools essential for the exploration and discovery of meaning in the self and events that lead the self into experiences. Consequently, the learner will be more ready to shape the situation than to be shaped by the situation in which he finds himself.

With the help of educators (and for the more deeply disturbed, psychiatrists and counselors) every person should have the opportunity to examine not only the wealthy storehouse of accumulated knowledge *about* the world, but how he personally can make constructive use of that knowledge both to make his own life more effective and to make the life around him more satisfying. To be an agent of change in this generation, a person must be ready to define the motives and goals that give his life direction. Again, he must be in touch with himself. His goals have the drawing power to determine the action and bring into question his motives. In experiential education, the learner develops his own goals (after he has considered his own desires and expectations). Action focused on future goals (not vague generalities, but concrete, specific, and measureable goals) can affect the learner markedly. The new behavior, bringing new satisfactions, can lead to new attitudes. It generally does not happen in the reverse.

Experiential education is goal-oriented. This fact alone assures that the teacher-learner is ready to learn, a basic condition for learning. Let me illustrate.

Several "learners" have arrived at the first teaching-learning session of a given course. The first hours are spent dealing with the learners' expectations and learning goals.

TEACHER-LEARNER: Experiential Learning is a laboratory learning process. I use this process here. I do not expect to teach *at* you. I expect that we will learn together. I believe we can teach each other, and that I can learn as a teacher and that you can teach as a learner.

A laboratory setting simply implies that within certain defined boundaries, we can work with several variables, unknowns, in the hope of discovering what these variables can do or mean to us in our lives. This, I hope, makes our learning both relevant and dynamic. In experimentation no attempt at an answer is wrong. We are free to try many things, even what appears to be ridiculous at first. Imagine Alexander Graham Bell thinking that he could talk across distances on a thin strand of wire. Ridiculous!

Now I'd like you to pair off, select a partner, and for the next few minutes discuss your answer to this question: What do you expect will happen in this class?

The teacher-learner pauses for five minutes, as the new learners interact.

Let me break through your discussion and invite you to move into quadrants (fours) of two pairs to continue your discussion, only using a minor shift in emphasis. Now discuss your answer to this question: What would you like to see happen in this class?

Again, there is interaction for five minutes.

Now bring two quadrants together, with one quadrant seated immediately behind the other. Like this:

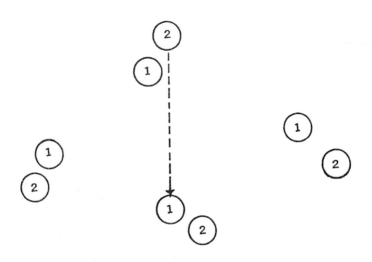

Let me give the first assignment to quadrant two. Your task now is to observe the person who is sitting directly across from you. Carefully consider the three questions listed before you as regards that person:
1. What does his role in his quadrant seem to be?
2. What does his central concern appear to be?
3. How might he be more helpful?

Remain silent during the next few minutes. You will have a chance to feed your information to your opposite after six or eight minutes of observation.

Here, the teacher-learner is beginning to initiate several important processes central to experiential education. Question one helps the observer and the observed to begin to look at roles each one plays in a group. This is a process question. Question two allows for a substantive (content) focus. What does he see as the task? Is he doing the task? Question three begins the personal feedback process which, if done gently, becomes a helpful first encounter that leads to personal growth and change.

Now let me speak to the first quadrant on the inside of the circle. You have been discussing both your expectations and your hopes for this course. Right now, I would like to encourage you to focus on what your personal learning goals are to be as they relate to this course. Simply put: What do you want to learn this term in this class? You will have six to eight minutes to discuss this question.

After the six to eight minutes of interaction, ask the observer to work with the observed (in pairs) in order to feed back the information gleaned during the first encounter.

Now, return to the same groups. Do not discuss what your observer told you, but use whatever your observer shared with you as you wish in the next four-minute encounter, as you bring to a close your discussion regarding your personal learning goals.

After four minutes, reverse the roles. Ask quadrant one to observe quadrant two in the same manner as before. Take the time to clarify the assignments.

When this process is completed, have the two quadrants merge into a single group. Suggest:

For the next ten minutes, discuss what you have heard from each other. Using newsprint (or the chalkboard), write down those personal learning goals your group feels are important to everyone in the group. You may have only one, or you may have as many as eight or nine. List them.

Have each group of eight post its list on the wall or board. Together, as a total group, examine all the goals and develop what seem to be the trends, until the group (not by eliminating the personal learning goals, all of which are valid) can highlight some of the more common goals. They should come to some consensus as to what goals the class can bring into focus for the work period that lies immediately ahead.

Having chosen common learning goals and having posted them explicitly, test the group commitment.

> Are you ready to dig into this/these area(s) of concern? Discuss together what you expect to contribute to this enterprise and what you expect others to contribute. Be specific.

This discussion can be conducted one to one, or in small groups of eight, or as a total group. It is important that these commitments be stated explicitly somewhere. It would be good to write them down. These commitments are what is known as a "contractual arrangement," essential to experiential learning. It is to say, "This I will commit myself to do during this period of time." It is a "buying-in" process that helps the learner to know that the learning to be done is his responsibility, not another's (i.e., teacher's).

In a church setting, this contractual arrangement is often called a "covenant." A covenant agreement generally includes:

1. a contractual agreement between specific persons, in a specific time;
2. an agreement upon objectives;
3. an agreement regarding the frame of reference (beliefs); and
4. an agreement regarding the guidelines (norms) for operation (bylaws).

Any time a new person joins the group, or a member leaves the group, the covenant-contract must be reexamined, and, if necessary, rewritten. Any time the group membership changes, the whole contractual arrangement changes. (This is one reason for every church to rewrite its covenant at the coming of every new minister.)

Now we have the basis for a teaching-learning experience.

There are three primary styles of experiential education: situational, structured, and contrived. Let us examine each style briefly:

Situational: In a very real sense, every experience we have is potential data for learning. Living every day, moving in and out of events and relationships, making and breaking commitments, success and failure, all serve as grist for growth. But most important is to be willing and disciplined enough to stop experiencing long enough to enter the learning process. Again, we are tempted simply to move from one activity to another, without explicit learnings. In every extraordinary situation, and periodically during the routine, someone needs to ask these questions: 1. What happened? 2. What was helpful? What was not helpful? 3. What have we learned that will help us another time?

Structured: Most classroom learning is structured. The classroom may be in the out-of-doors while trekking up Pike's Peak, sightseeing in New York City, or sailing in a sixty-foot ketch across the Gulf Stream from Florida to Bimini. It may be a schoolroom, or the hallway, or the auditorium. It might well be a playing field, or the auditorium stage, or the band rehearsal room. Structured learning can happen in a church school class, in the church council, in a counseling session, or in worship. What the word "structure" implies is not the place, but the deliberate effort of one or more persons to pull learnings from experiences, while, at the same time, he or they may seek to heighten the learning by structuring an added experience. This direction is generally done by the designated, but sanctioned, leader in a given group. But not always. Other leadership can emerge at specific times, be sanctioned by the group, and serve to facilitate significant learning.

What happens? The teacher-learner becomes spontaneously aware of something happening that is not seen directly by either the group or the individual to whom it is happening. In the hope of intensifying the data for instructional purposes, he may use an exercise, such as the action parable discussed in chapter 3.

Contrived: Since 90 percent or more of our teaching forces in public and private schools, in church schools, and in social agencies, tend to develop a teaching style that is contrived ("I must control what *my* pupil is learning"), the experiential learner must be prepared to pull learnings from even these experiences or lose great worlds of knowledge and wisdom. It is amazing, but people can learn under these conditions, not only *in spite of* the teacher, but *because* of the teacher. The real responsibility for learning lies with the learner anyway. To move through a contrived, gimmick-ridden, and controlled "learning" situation *is* an experience. The same questions need to be asked. What happened? What was helpful? What was not helpful? What can I learn (even about teaching) from this experience?

Learning occurs most easily when the learner is conscious of his necessary participation in the process. The joy of this truth is that we can learn from everything; and we can learn the most when:

We are responsible for our own learning.

We learn from our mistakes.

We learn from the mistakes of others.

We make the most out of our present condition.

Experiential education basically requires the development of specific here-and-now skills if a teacher-learner is really going to make it happen.

1. Experiential education encourages a *maximum participation.* First, each learner is responsible for his own learning. Second, each learner is encouraged to get involved since he will learn more by doing than by watching. (This is a serious matter for a learner who has been previously schooled in spectator education.) Third, each learner is helped to discover that the resources he brings to the learning experience are a part of the learning grist. Fourth, all learners are encouraged to build on each other's resources in the hope of finding new learning. Fifth, each learner is respected for who he is rather than for what he knows, freeing him from the congestive anxiety of questioning his self-worth. He knows that when his anxiety level goes up, his learning level goes down.

2. Experiential education encourages *respect for the person.* Contrary to the accusations of those who oppose the small group experiential education process, this style of education develops individuality; it does not deter it. It is a freeing process; supporting the person while he is exploring and discovering for himself new avenues of learning; helping the person to discover his own potential and ways he can develop it; and encouraging experimentation with the right to fail in the hope of growing. Experiential education does not threaten a man's right to be in control of himself, nor his right to control what affects his life. And it guarantees the same rights to others. This respect for the individual is certain only in community, a community where dependence is mature and voluntary.

3. Experiential education *applies the learnings of human development.* The process takes into serious account what the person can be expected to learn or achieve at his particular stage of life. It is fair and yet open to those who can achieve more and to those who, for various reasons, achieve less. The process enables the learner to set his own learning pace and to find his own primary learning style.

(Secondary and tertiary tools do not go undeveloped, but how the learner learns best is understood and fully developed.)

4. Experiential education applies all that we have learned about the *small group process*. The process takes into account not only the level of individual development but the level of group development. Since most of what happens to us happens in relationship to others, an understanding of the small group process helps to achieve a maximum level of learning as well as a maximum level of satisfaction. Successful use of this process requires both a theoretical and an experiential preparation. It also requires an understanding of what strengthens and what blocks group interaction, the roles group participants play, the development of decision-making tools for group life, and ways to develop group cohesion for mutual support and growth.

5. Experiential education leaves room for *shared leadership*. The designated teacher is acknowledged as a learner, too. As participants discover and come to respect their own resources, they are encouraged to use them to facilitate multiple learning in the learning community. No one is encouraged to lead all the time. No one is encouraged to follow all the time. The community moves toward a mutuality that encourages total commitment and a willingness to share.

6. Experiential education is a learning style that permits, indeed, symbolizes, *flexibility*. In a world of rapid change, no one idea becomes *the* idea. No one form holds all the answers. Spontaneity is the key to the learner's development (see chapter 4).

7. Experiential education is *personal goal oriented*. It depends on the will of the learner to learn, on his readiness to learn, and on his willingness to apply the learning. The teacher-learner may structure the opportunities for learning but only in the hope of the learner's responding.

8. Experiential education always *deals with living issues*. Even ancient history can be taught with a view for learnings applicable in our lives today. And what other reasons are there for studying it? To pile up knowledge? The teacher-learner teaches relevance, lives relevance, and aims to make the learning relevant for the learner.

3. THE ACTION PARABLE: EXPERIENTIAL EDUCATION IN A BIBLICAL SETTING

The leaders of the temple came to Jesus and one, a lawyer, asked him, "Who is my neighbor?" Spontaneously, Jesus turned to his questioner with a descriptive response, a parable of a worthy Samaritan. At the conclusion Jesus asked: "Which of these three, do you think, proved a neighbor to the man who fell among the robbers?" (Luke 10:25-37). The answer was obvious. "The one who showed mercy on him." Jesus turned his question into a learning experience. He used a dynamic process to teach an imperative kingdom principle. And those who were ready learned new behavior. The others? They were left to consider what he had said.

The "good" churchmen of Jesus' day were arguing one day about what could be legitimately done on the sabbath. Even Jesus' disciples were confused. Seeing one among them whose arm was withered, they asked, "Is it lawful to heal on the sabbath?" Jesus said: "What man of you, if he has one sheep and it falls into a pit on the sabbath, will not lay hold of it and lift it out? Of how much more value is a man than a sheep! So it is lawful to do good on the sabbath." Then he said to the man, "Stretch out your hand." And the man stretched it out, and it was restored, whole like the other (Matthew 12:9-13). Again, the answer to his question was obvious. The incident, through his question, was turned into another learning.

There was an important encounter between Jesus and his disciples. John recorded it when he reported Jesus to have said:

I am the true vine, and my Father is the vinedresser. Every branch of mine that bears no fruit, he takes away, and every branch that does bear fruit he prunes, that it may bear more fruit. You are already made clean by the word which I have spoken to you. Abide in me, and I in you. As the branch cannot bear fruit by itself, unless it abides in the vine, neither can you, unless you abide in me (John 15:1-4).

Still later Jesus says:

> As the Father has loved me, so have I loved you; abide in my love. If you keep my commandments, you will abide in my love, just as I have kept my Father's commandments and abide in his love. These things I have spoken to you, that my joy may be in you, and that your joy may be full. This is my commandment, that you love one another as I have loved you. Greater love has no man than this, that a man lay down his life for his friends. You are my friends . . . (John 15:9-14).

Once more, Jesus drew a likeness — only this time to the very in- carnation of the word itself. "I am the truth." And for those who had ears to hear, there was learning. Those who believed under- stood and drew nearer to learn from him what it meant to love.

The implications of the above encounters (and many more such encounters reflected in the Gospels) have a great deal to say to church educators working in today's explosive era of religious change. The warning of Jesus that "he who has ears to hear, let him hear" (Luke 8:8), is clear and relevant in our day. His uncanny ability to wed the substance to the right dynamic process made his teaching alive and exciting. Can we learn from his methods as well as his message?

Of all Jesus' teaching tools (preaching, healing, parables, demon- stration, discussion, ritual, drama, encounter, and interpretation) the parable, whether it was in an art form, an action form, or in his own modeling of behavior, was the most effective. The parable is a dynamic process that can lend itself appropriately to every occa- sion. In many encounters, when the direct, spoken word would have had no effect, Jesus refrained from directness. With a skill developed by one who is well disciplined in the art of communica- tion, Jesus focused upon the truth he desired to share. Spontaneously he sought the best medium for sharing it, allowing the hearer the prerogative of learning or not. On one occasion, he simply bent over the earth and wrote characters in the sand (see John 8:1-11). On another occasion, he sat the crowd down in circles of fifty, and fed them (see Mark 6:44). On another occasion he stood silently before his judge (see John 18:33-38a).

The response to him was varied. Some believed. They heard him gladly. There were those who were confounded by it all: skeptics. They saw little or no meaning in his words, actions, and life. For them, life found significance in concept, law, and principle — ab- stractions.

Others became hostile. And they were many. The learnings were far too close to the truth of their lives. They had worked too hard and too consciously to sublimate it. "God is light and in him is no darkness at all. If we say we have fellowship with him while we walk in darkness, we lie and do not live according to the truth . . ." (1 John 1:5-6). Those who live with hostility, or sentimentality, live with darkness. Jesus' confrontations created an internal conflict within the hearers: to be real or to be phony. To resolve the conflict meant change. And after spending so much time, money, and energy establishing a course of action that would help one cope with the world (if not solve one's problems), change would be too costly and painful, even if it meant being real. It would be better to silence this man of conscience than risk the encounter. Those who were hostile sought to silence him.

And there were those who felt that Jesus' instruction was folly. These were the hedonists and the Epicureans. "What's the good of it? Nothing will come of his cause. Like everything else that men have tried, it, too, will be tuned out. Can any good really come out of Nazareth?" This was the voice of the fatalists, the "eat, drink, and be merry" group. For them, life's meaning was found in temporary pleasures. Suffering was to be avoided at all cost.

Jesus confronted all these men in his parables. The parable seldom offended to the point of total rejection. It was grist for consideration.

The powerful descriptive words, the pungent act, the living model, were hard to erase in the mind of the hearer. They lingered with the hearer for months, even years. Later, the truth of the parable, under the right conditions, was often uncovered. The parable was a dynamic, free of contrivance and coercion. It left the learner free to learn for himself.

Three major categories of the parable are found in Jesus' life and ministry: (1) there is the *spoken parable,* or the art parable (2) there is the *action parable,* and (3) there is the fuller, more complete *parable of Jesus' life and modeled ministry.*

The *action parable* is closely related to both the art parable and the modeled parable. It serves really as the pivot form of parable between the words and the life of Jesus. The action parable affected the temple bureaucrat, the synagogue moderate, and the common citizen. Jesus' main concern was for the latter. The common citizen had become frustrated over the massive verbiage of the *Torah* and *Talmud.* The professional "clergy" insisted that to win God's favor one had to adhere to every jot and tittle of the law; an insistence that only the affluent could fulfill. To be "good" meant to commit all of the law to memory, and to have the freedom to live sufficiently apart from life's oppression so as to be free from gross error. Therefore Jesus addressed himself to the common citizen, not to the affluent. It was to the common citizen that Jesus hoped to make the gospel of salvation relevant. It was for the common citizen that he spoke in parables, healed the infirm, and lived a life of joy and service. His goal was made explicit:

"I came that they may have life, and have it abundantly" (John 10:10).

In his declaration of faith, John declared: "In him was life" (John 1:4).

The affluent received Jesus' most direct barbs (see Matthew 23). When the Pharisee, scribe, and priest addressed him as "good teacher," he responded abruptly with, "Why do you call me good? No one is good but God alone" (Luke 18:19).

The spoken parable is sometimes more difficult for the common citizen to interpret than the action parable, for the spoken parable requires a reflective skill that includes an open, searching mind, an awareness of the use of metaphor and simile. The action parable, on the other hand, requires little of this same skill, for it is more direct. It is, in fact, an encounter, a confrontation which involves all the senses: sight, hearing, smell, touch, and taste. It is multi-dimensional as a communication process. Therefore, it is more likely to communicate what is intended. In a very real sense it is hanging "flesh on the word" (cf. John 1:14).

The action parable is real, concrete, and observable. The word came to dwell among men. It defied the Gnostic assumption: "It can't be real!" The word is an actual event. It happens to somebody at sometime in someplace. It has implications that go far beyond the event, the person, or the place. It affects everything that follows — even if the event is as simple as a touch from one who hides in a crowd: "And a woman . . . came up behind him, and touched the fringe of his garment; and immediately her flow of blood ceased. And Jesus said, 'Who was it that touched me?'" (Luke 8:43-45). She had believed.

To the *confounded*, who work from a framework that does not agree that the "real" means the "concrete," but prefer the rational safety of the conceptual, the action parable is a stumbling block.

They must rationalize, excuse, or eliminate it. The *hostile* see the action parable as a threat. The *foolish* see the action parable as inconsequential. But the *believer* sees in it the "evidence of things not yet seen," giving new strength to his faith.

The parable as a teaching tool was intended for the unbeliever as well as for the believer. It speaks beyond the explicit, especially to those who are sensitive.

As a tool the parable is no less relevant in our day than it was in Jesus' day. It may be even more relevant. We all live at the edge of life's explosions — of population, technology, information, communication, and a dozen others. While we live, we must learn. While we learn, we must live. But how? Again, the action parable can be the pivot that brings the actual together with the reflective.

Jesus came to show us a new way of coping with this explosive life. Fearful, caught up in our own anxieties, and already adjusted to the ways of the old, we find it difficult to hear him, and to change, except verbally. In behavior we remain the same. Unless there is a way to show us what the new way is all about, a way that is more worthy of our life than the old way, we will not risk any new behavior. New learning necessitates the unlearning of the old. And that is difficult. We require some kind of supportive structure to help us while we learn the new. We need some place to practice our newfound behavior; to risk failure until the new becomes as familiar as the old was once. This support is not easy to find. That is why experiential education is rooted in the small group community process.

When I talk about a parable, what do I mean?

A parable is a spontaneous, descriptive, and relevant response to life as it is. It is a way of understanding life. It is a way of highlighting specific areas of life. Every parable has six characteristic factors that are in evidence. A parable:

1. is simple, single in its objective.
2. is concrete, descriptive in its nature.
3. is relevant, strongly attached to the hearer's daily life.
4. reflects the common life, but in an uncommon framework.
5. has many ramifications beyond the intended purpose.
6. leaves the response up to the learner.

If we review the parables of the stray sheep, the lost coin, and the prodigal son (Luke 15), we will see the basic factors suggested above reflected in these parables.

Let's apply this learning, then, to our explicit concern: the action parable. Do you remember when Jesus was confronted by a questioning group of disciples of John the Baptist? They had learned about religion from the harsh side of commitment — deprivation and fasting. Now, while John and disciples were given to fasting, Jesus was out celebrating, feasting, playing, and smiling. "Are you the one for whom we look, as promised? Or do we look for another?" they asked.

There were few words. Jesus simply turned to John's followers, pointed to those about him and said,

> Go and tell John what you hear and see: the blind receive their sight and the lame walk, lepers are cleansed and the deaf hear, and the dead are raised up, and the poor have good news preached to them. And blessed is he who takes no offense at me (Matthew 11:2-6).

What an encounter!

On another occasion, Jesus' reply to those who doubted him: "Believe me that I am in the Father and the Father in me; or else believe me for the sake of the works themselves" (John 14:11). He *did* heal. Those who responded *did* find new insight, new learning, new freedom, and new meaning in life. His actions were borne out of his commission as a chosen servant of God:

> The Spirit of the Lord is upon me,
> because he has anointed me to preach good news to the poor.
> He has sent me to proclaim release to the captives.
> and recovering of sight to the blind,
> to set at liberty those who are oppressed,
> to proclaim the acceptable year of the Lord.
> (Luke 4:18-19)

The consequence of Jesus' commitment was obvious. These people *were* free. The acts of Jesus incarnated his principles, his proclamation. THAT WAS DIFFERENT. THAT WAS NEW. THAT WAS THE GOSPEL. AND THAT IS THE ACTION PARABLE.

He healed — by touching.

He loved — by loving.

He created — by laboring.

He focused — by acting.

His life and his ministry were his most vital lesson.

"And the Word became flesh and dwelt among us" (John 1:14).

In surveying Jesus' healing ministry, it becomes evident that the same factors that are true of his spoken parables are also true of his action parables. These action parables are often experienced by others while Jesus used the occasion for teaching. (Not *all* of Jesus' action parables were recorded for us by the Gospel writers.)

1. They are simple, single in their objective.
2. They are concrete, dynamic in happening.
3. They are relevant to the need of the learner and meet him where he is.
4. They reflect the cry of the common life through an uncommon framework of caring.
5. There are as many ramifications to the action as to the thoughts.
6. The response is up to the learner.

The Gospel records a number of immediate instances of learning and healing:

"And he [Jesus] stretched out his hand and touched him, saying, 'I will; be clean'" (Matthew 8:3).

"He touched her hand, and the fever left her . . ." (Matthew 8:15).

"'If I only touch his garment, I shall be made well'" (Matthew 9:21).

". . . they might only touch the fringe of his garment; and as many as touched it were made well" (Matthew 14:36).

Some came *believing*. They found a new openness in their seeking that permitted exploration, discovery, and a new appropriation of new learnings. Some were *confounded*, skeptical that anything good could come out of Nazareth (let alone a Messiah). Others were *hostile*, feeling that the man severely threatened their well-established forms and institutions. Surely he must be demonic. Still others *laughed*, mocking him; for they could not believe that there was any God who cared for them. They continued either in revelry or misery, or both.

These actions of Jesus brought healing to the body, to the mind, and to the emotions. They affected the whole person. They resulted in changed behavior. They led to conversion. They ended in community.

Jesus healed a man by reaching the nerve that most needed to be reached, whether it was in the body, the mind, or the emotions. The ancient Greeks tended to separate the human being into various compartments, as we westerners do. But not Jesus. He saw man as a whole. The Gnostic tried to transform everything worthy of allegiance into an idea. But not Jesus. He saw man as more than an idea. The Jew attempted to localize salvation. Not Jesus. He saw man as a spirit. Jesus' theology is the theology of the abundant life, a theology of hope, a theology of relationship. His theology was the motivation of his action parables. They were always couched in the context of love. For Jesus, life from the beginning to the end was integrated by love. The action parable confirmed it, in the here and now. This is PRESENCE.

Let's look at it another way. If words (symbols) had the power to banish plagues, we would have been free of them long ago. Shakespeare showed the value of action when he had Hamlet set out to prove what he insightfully knew: his uncle murdered his father to marry his mother and take over the kingdom. Hamlet knew that the king was hiding behind the diplomatic sham of words. With some cunning, Hamlet plotted with the king's players for an event (similar to a psychodrama) that would mirror what Hamlet suspected to be the truth of the crime. By this device, he expected to disclose his uncle's guilt. With a conscious expectancy (and with a boyish excitement) Hamlet exclaimed:

> . . . the play's the thing
> Wherein I'll catch the conscience of the king.[2]

Shakespeare, it was evident, was aware of the games people play with words. They use them to confound, to manipulate, to project, to hide, to avoid, to justify, to vindicate, to subjugate, and to injure. It is little wonder that those who follow the trail of Marshall Mc-Luhan rule that the written and spoken word are forms of communication of the lowest common denominator. The written word can be construed to mean whatever the reader desires. The spoken word is dependent upon the intonations, not only of the speaker, but of the hearer. The individual's own feelings may keep him from fully learning all of the message. To be effective, the communication media must be expanded. The more senses one uses to get his message across, the more likely he is to communicate his intention.

This fuller style of communication requires a new kind of leadership, the kind of leadership that can and will make use of the action-parable style of learning. Action parables are more than exercises, more than "games." An action parable is used to reveal a truth, descriptively and dynamically. Like anything else, it can be ex-

---

[2] William Shakespeare, *Hamlet,* act 2, scene 2, lines 633-634.

ploited. But only in an actualized relationship based on trust can another discover God's greatest gift to man: relationship.

1. *The new leader must know himself.* One of the realities seen in Jesus' life was that he always made a conscious use of himself in every situation. In short, he was in control of himself — disciplined — in prayer, in study, in relationship, in encounter, and on the cross. He knew who he was, whom he served, and where he was going.

The Socratic claim that the highest good is to "know thyself" finds a ring of truth in Jesus. To the Christian, however, this truth goes further: "To know God is to know oneself." That is not to be construed to mean that self and God are one-and-the-same. It simply means that to know God is to reveal what it is to be human. To be a new kind of leader in using the action parable, it is imperative to make a conscious use of the self. This suggests the same awareness and ability to take control of the self (not others) and use the self to the best advantage in every condition in life; with one's family, in one's vocation, in one's social contacts, and in helping others. Being thoroughly human means weighing sentiment against hardness of heart, and discovering somewhere in between real compassion. It means weighing absolutism against promiscuity in the hope of discovering love. It means being able to say, with some sense of trust, I AM, without apology, role-dependence, or excuse. It means also that one is ready to expose himself for the sake of genuine communication: to speak the truth in love.

2. *The new leader must develop the skills* necessary to be spontaneous. How hard it is to apply ourselves to the long arduous task of disciplined skill development. But the leader who finds this new action-parable style to his liking is one who has pulled together a disciplined set of actions that include: (a) an understanding of individual human development, (b) an understanding of group development and group dynamics, (c) an understanding of the leader's role, (d) an understanding of administrative techniques, (e) a willingness to keep records (in some order), (f) an openness to research and development, and (g) an openness to other cooperative efforts, especially from the other helping disciplines.

And what is more, he internalizes these skills. He travels with none of the previously needed excess baggage which tends to limit him. He is ready to appropriate whatever is necessary for the present situation. He is not afraid to test everything, nor to be tested. He will not avoid the here and now. He finds Christianity a way, a process, a movement; not a shackle. Structure becomes a temporary vehicle; needed, but not ultimate.

3. *The new leader must know what he is doing.* The skilled leader needs to know more than the technical details of what he is doing. He needs to know the theory behind the action and the consequences anticipated. He needs to practice the action that manifests the theory, and he needs adequate correctives which will check out the reliability of his judgment.

4. *The new leader must have supervised practice* in learning what tools to use appropriately. So many negative events happen while a leader is using good tools in the wrong way at the wrong time. Advancement and use of these tools is often blocked, permanently, because of one bad experience resulting from poor timing or poor judgment, or both. An innovation needs to be tried and weighed. Carefully supervised action in which all persons are mutually informed can lead to successful experimentation in new forms of learning without harmful side effects. The informed serve as their own corrective agents.

5. *The new leader must be conscious of many of the ramifications* that can develop from his actions. Everything he does to and with people affects them for good or ill. Some leaders have said that poor leadership really doesn't hurt anybody. I'm not sure that the world says that about Hitler's leadership of Germany prior to and during World War II. We need checks and balances. Those who resist innovation are a serious part of that check and balance system. This is to say, they should not be dismissed too easily. They should be heard, for they represent that force which guarantees our society some stability that the innovator, out of necessity, cannot offer.

6. *The new leader needs to be human.* He needs to accept the human role that is his. To lay claim upon one's own "god-ness," like Alexander the Great, is a testimony to his own depravity as a man.

4. THE THEOLOGY FOR CHANGE

Then Jesus was led up by the Spirit into the wilderness to be tempted by the devil. And he fasted forty days and forty nights, and afterward he was hungry. And the tempter came and said to him, "If you are the Son of God, command these stones to become loaves of bread." But he answered, "It is written, 'Man shall not live by bread alone, but by every word that proceeds from the mouth of God.'"

Then the devil took him to the holy city, and set him on the pinnacle of the temple, and said to him, "If you are the Son of God, throw yourself down; for it is written, 'He will give his angels charge of you,' and 'On their hands they will bear you up, lest you strike your foot against a stone.'" Jesus said to him, "Again it is written, 'You shall not tempt the Lord your God.'"

Again, the devil took him to a very high mountain, and showed him all the kingdoms of the world and the glory of them; and he said to him, "All these I will give you, if you will fall down and worship me." Then Jesus said to him, "Begone, Satan! for it is written, 'You shall worship the Lord your God and him only shall you serve.'"

Then the devil left him, and behold, angels came and ministered to him.

. . . Jesus began to preach, saying, "Repent, for the kingdom of heaven is at hand" (Matthew 4:1-11, 17).

From the earliest moments of Jesus' ministry, it was apparent that this new gospel was based upon a new sense of what theology is. That is not to say that Jesus was without his own struggle for insight and decision. He did struggle, in the manner evidenced above. But he had found a vital affirmation from God, "This is my beloved Son, with whom I am well pleased" (Matthew 3:17). He was aware of his call and the urgency of his mission. John the Baptist was courting trouble with the high powers. He would soon be silenced. Jesus' wilderness question was a serious one, "I know the message; by what media shall I proclaim it?" It was as if he, too, was certain that the media had to complement the message in order to be heard.

Like so many pilgrims deciding on a way, he withdrew to the solitude of a wilderness (which speaks more strongly of his confusion among alternatives and his frustration in the face of decision than of a place somewhere in Palestine). The discipline of fasting forced him into a fuller contact with all of himself, both conscious and unconscious; enabling his whole being to reach out to God. (There may be an analogy to his fasting in the contemporary mystic's sojourn into prolonged meditation, sharing in a marathon experience, or entering a covenant relationship of some intensity for a given period of time.) He struggled to get in touch with God's way, in the hope that what he had been called to do would, indeed, initiate the kingdom.

In effect, Jesus considered assuming the messianic mission in various proposed roles, all functional: A mighty warrior? A political power? A mystical religionist with strange powers?

No, not one of these roles was adequate to bring into being what he felt God had in mind: an eternal kingdom. The functional was meant to be temporary, more the mood of survival than the mood of service. And after a time, following John's arrest, Jesus came out of the wilderness preaching, "Repent, for the kingdom of heaven is at hand" (Matthew 4:17).

His cry for repentance was not new — for John had made it quite clear that salvation was only for those who would return to God as the author and finisher of their lives. The call was explicitly to convert, to change one's behavior, to renew one's commitment. No, this call was not new. But the destiny to which that cry for repentance called a man, that was new. And he spent his three-year ministry modeling its newness. For him, the kingdom meant community; the community of pilgrims, men and women who found God in their own love-union. God's greatest gift in Jesus Christ was the revelation made explicit in his incarnation: God is the God of relationship.

As a pilgrim on our journey, I move from intimacy to intimacy (from birth to death), and all the while, I seek continually for that intimacy. It is to be found, in this world, only in the recesses of a covenant community where every man has both a strong sense of belonging and an explicit sense of self-identity, both resting on trust.

All of life, whether it be viewed in faith as resting on God or in faith that there is no God, rests on a single faith assumption.

There is no calculable evidence for any other reality. Life is lived primarily in response to one or the other TRUST assumption:

There is a God — I am loved. I trust.

There is no God — I am afraid. I cannot trust.

Building from these basic affirmations, having chosen one or the other, two immediate survival characteristics demand our conscious (or unconscious) attention. The first is INTIMACY. (I put this first because I believe the second comes essentially as a response to the first, though they are mutually essential to each other.) This, in lay terms, is simply the affirmation: "I belong." The second is IDENTITY. In the world where "I belong" I am called into being by others who encounter or respond to me as a person. In this act, I know that "I am." This I need to affirm continually.

All three factors — trust, intimacy, and identity — are essential for human survival. If we do not find them legitimately, then we must substitute less legitimate forms to temporize our sense of well-being. Let me risk a judgment by inferring that 95 to 98 percent of all persons live without a legitimatized existence. This claim is the same as saying that 95 to 98 percent of us live as if there is no God. We do not really trust that others will or can affirm us. We seek and rely on substitutes. This has never been more apparent in the world than in our age of horrendous addictive behavior: drugs (including alcohol and tranquilizers), stimulants (including coffee and pills), compulsive action, impulsive living, uncommitted marriages, materialistic pursuit, Oedipus complexes — they all add up to "I must save myself." We are caught up in a wild orgy of competitive drudges who have settled on a "win/lose" track of interaction. Lined out, the theory looks like Diagram A, Column 1.

I speak of God within the framework of the Christian faith: God IS love (relationship). Essentially, Jesus expressed in word, action, and being, a God who, in his loving, affirms us as persons and as community. This affirmation we celebrate in our worship; we communicate in our mission; and we make immanent in our behavior. The promised kingdom lies in the love relationship. We see this explicitly in the events that immediately followed the wilderness experience of Jesus: he came out of the wilderness preaching, "Repent, for the kingdom of heaven is at hand." The blind were given sight. The deaf began to hear. The lame walked. The lepers were cleansed. And the poor heard the good news. Salvation was for all.

To some, God was only for the chosen ones who focused upon a

DIAGRAM A

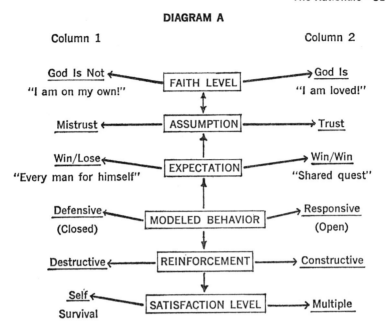

Column 1   Column 2

God Is Not ← "I am on my own!"	FAITH LEVEL	→ God Is "I am loved!"
Mistrust ←	ASSUMPTION	→ Trust
Win/Lose ← "Every man for himself"	EXPECTATION	→ Win/Win "Shared quest"
Defensive ← (Closed)	MODELED BEHAVIOR	→ Responsive (Open)
Destructive ←	REINFORCEMENT	→ Constructive
Self ← Survival	SATISFACTION LEVEL	→ Multiple

single geographic and historic place (localized in Jerusalem). He was, for others, the remainder of a long-lost promise: prosperity and prestige would return to the Jew. In the years that followed the division of Israel, through the invasion and dispersion of the Jewish people, the prophetic voices brought a message of hope in the inference that God was not to be seen geographically, nor nationally, but as one who governed all men in the universe. But they were, as the Scripture records time and again, only "voices crying in the wilderness." They went unheeded, if not unheard. The people heard the haunting din of the glorious memory of prosperity and prestige. For many of them, the realization of this memory would be the coming of the kingdom.

But Jesus proclaimed that God is not the God of the privileged, nor is he the God of any geographic or nationalized people. If there was any special role for the Jew in God's plan, it was a servant role. "God is spirit," said Jesus, "and those who worship him must worship in spirit and truth" (John 4:24).

Two additional texts of Jesus are of crucial importance: "I am . . . the truth . . ." (John 14:6). "You will know the truth, and the truth will make you free" (John 8:32). Once more, Jesus sets his theology, his mission, and his ministry in a relational context in a way which is suggestive of his sense of the whole. To the Greek, life was viewed through the maze of the mind, in parts. What gods there were, were the gods of many ideas. The mind read into every condition an ultimate purpose and a rational reason for being. The myths of Mount Olympus justified every action reported to be the actions of men. Men found it easier to be philosophic about life than to discipline the whole person. The separation of the body, the mind, and the spirit served to compartmentalize and, therefore, make more livable a life whose parts were often in conflict with each other. To the Greek, "god" was an idea. And like any other idea, it was a tool in the minds of the craftsman. The ability and the motives of the craftsman were often more important than the truth revealed to him.

There are some who even now espouse this Greek philosophy within the Judeo-Christian world. It is a convenient religious framework. It does explain much, and keeps God objectively "out there" somewhere. There is a kind of worship in this framework, but it is not very visceral. There is little evident relationship between what one "worships" in church and what one "lives" in the street. The rational call is for a cerebral religion. No emotion. No politics. No social reform. No counseling. "Don't mix religion and life."

The whole Gospel According to John, and likewise the Epistles of John, expose this Gnostic idealization of life. "God is spirit, and those who worship him must worship in spirit . . ." (John 4:24). By spirit, Jesus meant the inbreathing of life that fills the whole being. There is no separation: body, mind, and spirit. When Jesus talked about man, he talked about him as a single entity. He did not, indeed would not, compartmentalize him. Such a tragic separation of the parts led to illness, blindness, and derangement. Through the integrating power of love healing could take place.

Once more, Jesus met the claim of another major faith with the claims of his theology of relationship: God is love. He is *not* a geographic or national hex. He is not an idea. He is relationship.

God's being exists within the very nature of man: "God is at work in you, both to will and to work for his good pleasure" (Philippians 2:13).

God is not merely *a* relationship. *God is relationship.* "Love" and "relationship" are interchangeable here, for love is a relationship; and there is no real complete relationship without love. The Spirit of God makes that relationship possible (acknowledged or unacknowledged).

At this juncture, it becomes imperative to clarify two very important facets of relational theology: the substantive and the dynamic; in other words, the essence and the process. In this clarification we are faced with a paradox. Substantively, God is love and therefore, "the same yesterday, today, and forever." Dynamically, God is love and therefore, never the same – he is always moving. Can God be both? When we examine the message (LOVE) and the medium (MOVEMENT) separately, there is little concern or question. But when we link them together, "the medium is the message," then we must note them as paradoxical, but necessary to each other. God is both never changing and forever changing. The evidence lies in the incarnate nature of relationship.

Jesus was always unpredictable in his behavior; spittle for a healing experience, a whip for a confrontation, patterns drawn in the sand, deliberate neglect of his pleading family, and a committed trek toward Jerusalem. Every meeting was fresh and new. But in every encounter, Jesus' love came through.

A theology of relationship is an entwining of the substantive and the dynamic, the interpersonal and the functional. It is the model from which all human life seeks its meaning.

Everyone of us operates through life on two tracks, usually developing more concern and skill in one area than another. One track is the pragmatic, functional track of human need. "I must learn a skill and work in order to eat." The second track I call the interpersonal, the aesthetic track. This facet of life generally spices up the first track of life and gives life its meaning. Both need a full and conscious development by the person who wants to lay hold of the eternal life which lays a primary emphasis on the second track.

Unfortunately, to save ourselves, we generally give the emphasis to the first, the functional track. Our lives grow dim with sameness, boredom, and emptiness; but at least we survive.

But to live only in the second sphere, the interpersonal, without considering the first, is to play the games of children. For an adult, this style can be called either promiscuity or psychosis.

For example, in good marriages partners bring complementary

characteristics together and help each other as pilgrims in search of intimacy, to develop a more balanced life, functional and interpersonal. If the husband is pragmatic (functional), and therefore tends to be dominant, and if the wife is more aesthetic (interpersonal), and therefore a little less dominant, a realization that these factors complement each other can assist a couple in developing a happy, creative relationship. At first, the encounters tend to suggest to the couple a basic incompatibility (much like all paradoxes, as "God is always the same, and never the same"). This contrast leads to stress, worry, and sometimes premature separations. With some deliberate work, this "incompatibility" can become a "complementing."

Jesus modeled a theology of relationship essential and relevant to all areas of life in our world today. This is a theology for change. It is a strange mixture of psychology, sociology, ethics, economics, and all the other considered disciplines of life. Is it so strange that a theology should catch up all that is valid from both the vertical and the horizontal factors in life? It should not be. For in Jesus we have a wedding of both in the Incarnation and the Resurrection.

Now let us examine four important facets of this theology for change in light of four basic applied behavioral science principles: (1) the here and now, (2) process, (3) subjectivism, and (4) personhood. Theologically, the counterbalance looks as follows:

Here and Now. Presence
Process .... Encounter
Subjectivism .. Truth
Personhood ... The Full Life

1. THE HERE AND NOW . . . PRESENCE

If God is not a geographic place, and if God is not an idea, and if God is relationship, then God must be both destructible and indestructible. In him lie both the Incarnate (destructible) and the Resurrection (indestructible). To be both, God must make the mystery of his being known in the five dimensional, concrete senses and yet not be either material or wholly immaterial. He must be knowable and unknowable. Hence, he is no God of brass and gold, nor an abstraction of some gameful mood. He is Presence.

Why is this concept so strange?

Is not man, who is made in his image, the same? Man is so knowable and yet so unknowable. He is so predictable and yet so unpredictable. Every moment is a revelation out of the exciting moment of the man. This is what makes marriage so exciting. The wife we felt we knew; the husband we considered predictable; becomes renewed, more re-created from time to time, and what we felt was fixed is in motion again. And if there is any hope in developing the relationship further, with a full consideration of what has been, and in light of what one hopes, both work together NOW and make it all come about. After all, we only have the now.

The key to this kind of existentialism lies in our understanding of the basic germ of life: SPONTANEITY. Let me take the time now to define the word since it is used constantly by the behavioral scientist and the relational theologist. Spontaneity means action that is without external constraint or stimulus. The person acts out of his own free will, voluntarily, either taking the initiative or responding to someone else's initiative. Spontaneity is controlled internally. In general, it is *natural* action, not without similarity to the actions of children, to which Jesus referred when he spoke to his disciples:

> And they were bringing children to him, that he might touch them; and the disciples rebuked them. But when Jesus saw it he was indignant, and said to them, "Let the children come to me, do not hinder them; for to such belongs the kingdom of God. Truly, I say to you, whoever does not receive the kingdom of God like a child shall not enter it." And he took them in his arms and blessed them, laying his hands upon them" (Mark 10:13-16).

Too often the natural is deliberately restrained in favor of what appears to be a "better way." Is there a better way to relate than in the way of little children? Having lost our innocence in gaining knowledge, it is no longer easy to remain in such innocence. We strain to remain spontaneous.

Spontaneity carries with it three basic ingredients that the less innocent fear: immediacy, discipline, and conflict.

Immediacy is that which is occurring in the here and now. One cannot hang on to the past, or even, for that matter (like the millennialist) to the future. One lives only in the here and now. He cannot save up ready-made responses (clichés) in some great reservoir somewhere to be used for each critical occasion he will face. He must act, out of his inward parts, in the now.

Discipline. How does such a word ever find a justifiable spot in consideration of spontaneity? Perhaps it is best understood by a comparison with the impulsive/compulsive nature of most in our present-day humanity; a less natural style of behavior (neurotic) that chooses, by default, to live without internal discipline, but under external restraint. Discipline, therefore, is not the hard, rigorous limiting, found straining under the law. Laws are for those who do not know how to limit themselves. Discipline is a preparation of the self: an awareness, a skill, and an openness to encounter. For example, a disciplined medical doctor is one who has so internalized his own self-awareness and his medical skills that, when the occasion warrants, he is ready to function immediately, with wisdom and efficiency.

Conflict. To the spontaneous, conflict is expected. Wherever any innovation occurs, those who are most affected are threatened. Even those who trust find innovation threatening. The innovator creates new rules for living. Those acted upon need to be wary of the "once-in-a-lifetime" happening that has just occurred and may never occur again. Hence, they attempt to set external limits upon the spontaneous person. What they have newly experienced may be the work of an exploiter or a fool. It needs to be tested. The spontaneous person leads out again with understanding. He knows that initial resistance is both desirable and healthy.

There are very few adult persons who are spontaneous. For the most part, we are an addicted people, a people who have sought temporary alternatives to an eternal problem: pain as opposed to pleasure.

To test out the degree of spontaneity that exists in a group, the following action parable may be used. (Such a group would be more than simply a social meeting or interest group meeting.)

> SETTING: After an initial warm-up time (the exercise is not to be used at the first two or three meetings of the group), ask for three volunteers to help you in a brief experiment that can test the spontaneity level of the person. Dismiss these three persons, asking them to wait to be called one at a time. They should wait in a place where they cannot hear the procedures that will take place in the room.
>
> PREPARATION: Request the remaining group members to assist in this experience by being conscious of four basic elements in the action:
>
> 1. *Timing.* How much time does it take before the subject begins to react to the conditions suggested by the director? What significance does this have?
> 2. *Movement.* Does the subject move quickly? Deliberately? Slowly? With uncertainty? Does he move at all? Or does he tend to internalize? Verbalize?

3. *Values.* What is important to the subject? Why?
4. *Response.* What is the subject's response? Why does he respond that way? Is there a personal history that suggests the reason for his freezing? Internalizing? Verbalizing? Or acting?

DRAMATIC SYNOPSIS (The leader says to first subject after he has been called into the room, and each subject successively): "We are going to try an experiment together. Forget the rest of the group. They will try to help you by suggesting responses but will not interfere with the process. Whatever I tell you, respond imaginatively AS IF THAT WHICH I AM TELLING YOU IS ACTUALLY HAPPENING RIGHT AT THIS MINUTE. For example: If I were to tell you that the drape over there was in flames, you would react to the drape as if it really were aflame. Are you with me?" *(After getting a positive response, continue.)*

"Right now, you are sitting in a car *(place two chairs in center of group)* next to your wife (husband). *(Is he sitting in the car now? Driving?)* There are two teenagers in the rear seat jabbering away continuously. You are returning from a day's picnic at the church campground and feel somewhat "done in." You are on a very steep downgrade that swings into a left-hand curve. You know the narrow road rather well. At the end of the incline, where the road swings left, there is a high cliff and a deep reservoir at its foot, extending out a number of miles.

"There is a car in front of you with two adults (man and woman) and two children (boy and girl) with their family dog, obviously having a good time after a day's outing. Suddenly the car in front of you goes out of control and heads for the cliff. There are screams. *(Pause.)* The car swerves, crashes, and plunges into the reservoir. *(Pause.)* The screams continue. *(What is happening?)* The children cry: 'Save our dog. Save our dog.' The mother shouts, 'Save my children. Save my children!' The father cries, 'Help, I can't swim!' *(Pause.)* The car begins to sink. *(Pause.)* More cries! The water is up to the edge of the door. It's sinking. More screams. *(Pause. What is happening now? Is the subject thinking about it? Verbalizing what he would do? Or acting?)* The car is beginning to disappear under the water." *(Pause.)*

Have the subject join the group without any comment and invite the other two subjects in, one at a time, to experience the same event.

When all three have had their turns, you may want to begin either with the subjects or the group in asking for feelings, insights, and present thoughts. What happened? How did it happen? How did you feel? When you saw it happen the second or third time were your responses different? How did the observers feel? Did they want to yell out, "Move, man . . . move"? Check the movement, the values. (Did the subject want to save the dog first? The children? The woman? The husband?) Did he send for help? Did he stop the car he was in before getting out? Did he consider his own swimming ability? How did he respond?

This is a simulated situation which does not necessarily demon-strate what the person would do in a real situation. It simply demonstrates, in an exciting way, ways of reacting to critical situations. It brings into focus the whole question of spontaneous response.

How do you respond to critical situations? Are you spontaneous? Or are you programmed? Basically, you can respond in one of four broad ways: (1) paralyzed — frozen by unresolved fears, (2) computerized — "This is the way we have always done it!" (3) verbalized — "Let's discuss it." (4) actualized — "The play is the thing." The ACTION PARABLE favors the actualized response (4). The media heightens one's awareness and sensitivity. Each respondent tests his own capacity to feel and sense others and the condition of his environment.

In summary, spontaneity is the essence of faith's response to man and man's response to faith. It reflects the "God is at work within you" idea. It is imperative to a relational theology.

2. PROCESS . . . ENCOUNTER

Relationships are never sterile or stagnant. They are dynamic, moving, changing. People encounter. Jesus expressed it when he claimed "I am the way!" He modeled the behavior he expected from others. He encountered.

His encounters were not with those who agreed with him alone. Indeed, even those who followed him met his anger. "Get behind me, Satan!" (Mark 8:33). His most avid followers were sometimes his most difficult problems. They wanted too much for him; that is, a kingship he declined to acknowledge:

Who, though he was in the form of God, did not count equality with God a thing to be grasped, but emptied himself, taking the form of a servant, being born in the likeness of men (Philippians 2:6-7).

Again, the substance remained constant, but the dynamic was permitted to flow anew. And God was in the movement — a moving being. Life is a process — becoming. Man is a pilgrim — seeking being and becoming, and wanting to belong. Being — becoming — belonging can be affirmed only in encounter, where you can be the initiator *or* the respondent. Both are intimately and inextricably *involved*.

3. SUBJECTIVISM . . . TRUTH

In Jesus' statement "I am . . . the truth" (and others that bear upon it), we have the denial of what the man of the street so readily declares as truth: objective fact. To the functionalist, objective fact (if there is such a thing) is that which occurs "out there," can be grasped, defined, controlled, exploited, and cast off when finished.

To view personal relationships as such objective facts is to invert the intended will of the God of relationship. Making a person an "it" reflects the "itness" of the one who makes him so. When a person uses another as an object, he runs the risk of depersonalizing himself also. A subject (I) can only address another subject (Thou) and get response. The alternative is a hodgepodge of reaction.

A relational theology, then, is a theology that is highly subjective and the subjective, existential as it is, becomes all the truth (in love) we have. People, then, become the criteria for all our action and interaction.

Again, we have to move beyond the petty devices we use as our escapes. We have to risk the pain inevitable in the real world of encounter. To the functionalist (by design or by default) this reality threatens his illusion that "God is in his heaven, all is well with the world."

Remember Job?

In his enthusiasm for life, he became certain of his own success and sanction. He was indignant when the "plagues" hit his house and person. "How dare God do this to me, a faithful man?" That is to say, "Who does God think he is, to depose me of my kingdom?" Haven't you heard something like this said to you at one time or another? Or have you said it? The indignation of a self-righteous man, who had played "Jr. God" for many a year and has never moved outside of the functional sphere where partial, but not full, living is sometimes fully permitted, is often in error.

> Then the Lord answered Job out of the whirlwind:
> "Who is this that darkens counsel by words without knowledge?
> Gird up your loins like a man,
>   I will question you, and you shall declare to me.
> "Where were you when I laid the foundation of the earth?
>   Tell me, if you have understanding.
> Who determined its measurements — surely you know!
>   Or who stretched the line upon it?"
>
> (Job 38:1-5)

Job, as we, needed to learn humility.

DIAGRAM B

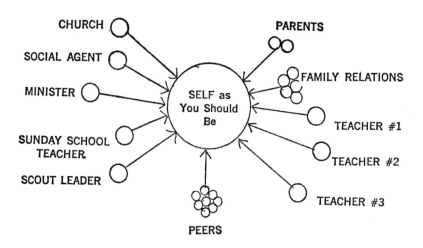

What happens to most of us, as our spontaneity is more and more restricted and mass production replaces personal creativity, is that a number of self-appointed committees composed of parents, siblings, relatives of various sorts, teachers, ministers, scout leaders, strong peers, and social agents pour into us as into children an image known popularly as the "ideal." It is a composite picture of everyone's "shoulds." "You *should* be everything good, positive, worthwhile, competent, controlling, and helpful." The person who does his work, doesn't ask too many questions, and behaves himself without much direction becomes the norm. Anything negative or disabling is eliminated. This gives us the halo effect. We are good . . . for everyone else who cannot be that good. This sounds positive, but it is debilitating. It is debilitating because it is an illusion not unlike the illusion of Adam, who felt that a little knowledge could make him God. Afraid to disappoint our self-appointed committees, we reach further and further into the illusion in the hope of some release.

But release never comes, as Diagram C shows. In an illusory world (fantasy) everything returns to its source. There we are both God, the Creator, and the object, the created. Our cry for help goes unheeded because it is unheard. We race into one activity

DIAGRAM C

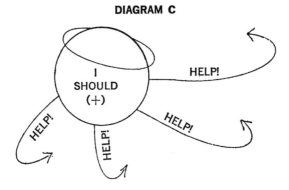

after another, hoping for some relief only to be doubly pressed again to keep up the pace or disappoint everyone. Somewhere in the hidden recess of the self we keep a well-hidden pocket of despair where all the less positive feelings are kept: resentment, loneliness, and desperation. We nurse it and coddle it regularly. Only the most closely related persons ever glimpse its contents (usually our spouse and children). We try never to expose it to the light. (D)

DIAGRAM D

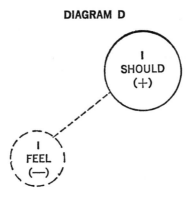

Let me put this concept in specifics. As children we are told over and over, "We must not hurt people's feelings. If you can't say anything nice, don't say anything at all!" We are taught to spend the positives, and bury what appears to be disabling (E).

What happens?

DIAGRAM E

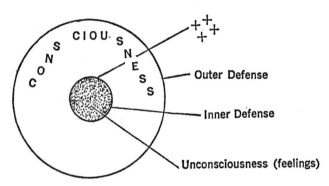

DIAGRAM F

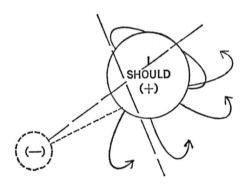

DIAGRAM G

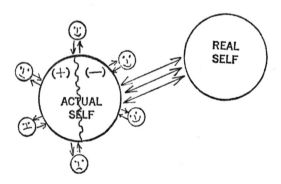

We end up spending all our "good" and withholding all our "bad." ("Good" and "bad" are in quotes because these words are society's way of defining these feelings, not mine.) We have a ready reservoir of hostility and no reserve of joy. The inner defense system thickens (we become more closed) and the conscious life is narrowed in fear of risking exposure to an unknown role or roles. Relationships are always functional. (We use each other.) They are seldom interpersonal. (We enjoy each other.) Our loneliness in our illusion, thanks to our committees, increases our problem. We intensify our efforts to find release and only go deeper into the abyss.

The alternative is to smash the illusion (Diagram F) that the "should" way is the actual, and begin the process of entering actuality again. The movement toward the "should" was the hope of winning the approval of all our committees (to please everyone) who by now have left us to fend for ourselves against the internalized forces that are a residue of all their expectations.

The process is painful for two reasons. First, we must leave the protected sphere of an already predetermined image (identity) and risk an encounter in the real world where we must fashion a new identity in relationship to others. Jesus did this. He was not satisfied to consider himself as "one with God." He took on "the likeness of man." To incarnate love, we have to risk an openness that exposes us to everyone. Our inner defenses must be diminished.

This leads us to the second level of pain. We are left alone to move into this new sphere of seeking: to seek out new community support, and to establish a new criteria for valuing life. This suspended period is a time of severe testing, and few cross it successfully. We find it easier to move back to "what we know" rather than risk the unknown in a highy subjective world. Here, a theology of relationship is absolutely essential to a community of fellow believers who want to be supportive of another pilgrim's struggle to leave his addictive behaviors and reach for love's eternal intimacy.

In Diagram G, those persons stationed around the convert are noted as the support group. The arrows moving in and moving out from him indicate a continual dialogue that leads to new understanding. "This is who I think I am!" "Who am I to you?"

In actuality, any person is not all "good." There are factors in all of us that can be labeled as strengths or desirable qualities (skills,

DIAGRAM H

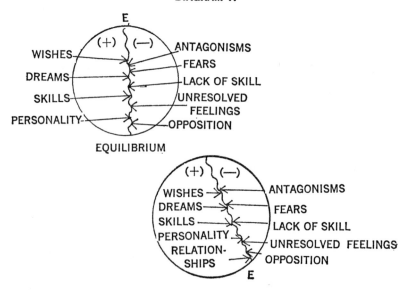

EQUILIBRIUM

personal character, values, motivation, etc.) and blocks or undesirable qualities (restraints, fears, resentments, etc.). Both kinds of factors are accepted, not denied. In fact, the blocks tend to be brought back into perspective so that in their resolve, the person's strengths may be really set free. Diagram H illustrates this personal "force-field." The strengths meeting the blocks create a personal equilibrium. Our tendency is to give an added thrust to our strengths (+) without any recognition to our blocks (−). This extra thrust tends to reinforce the block, which is a neurotic defense in the first place, intensifying the internal struggle and bringing no resolve.

Jesus reversed these tendencies. He put it this way:

> . . . If you are offering your gift at the altar, and there remember that your brother has something against you, leave your gift there before the altar and go; first be reconciled to your brother, and then come and offer your gift (Matthew 5:23-24).

The early church caught his message: ". . . confess your sins to one another . . ." (James 5:16).

In a trusted community of fellow pilgrims, there is release from these worldly neurotic blocks. The power of the subjective theology of relationship is the power of openness. With the blocks released, the strengths flow more easily, shifting the equilibrium, and giving a person great satisfaction in being what he is — human. There is no need for escape, for there are no impossible expectations that diminish his effectiveness with anxiety.

The desire to fulfill our true destiny creates a tension between what we are and what we can become. It is a creative tension, essential to our self-development. It motivates and evaluates our present action. It does not debilitate us. ("I can never attain that.") The promise was, "What I am, you can be, and more" (see Luke 24:44-49; Acts 1:4-8). As our self-actualizing progresses toward our goal, our goal also moves out and enlarges. As we grow, our vision grows. The creative tension continues to exist.

This growth is only possible in a subjective framework of human interaction, in relationship to others. The alternative is emptiness, loneliness, and despair.

4. PERSONHOOD . . . . THE FULL LIFE

"I am life" said Jesus. (See John 1:4; 5:21; 14:19; Romans 6:8; 1 Corinthians 15:22; Philippians 1:21; 1 John 5:12.) If we are as fully human as possible, not in spite of the tension but because of it, we are able to realize contentment in who we are and what we do under God. Affirmation in the actual is possible. Openness becomes its own constructive reward.

I have known fleeting moments of this personal freedom. Having lived for a time condemned under the whip of my tyrant "should," having found release from its hold in time to make some creative moves toward resolve and a happy application to my life, I hold firmly to the tensions, knowing that, in community, there is support for me when I grow weary. I am continually affirmed, even as I am exposed. This is not the same thing as saying, "I am right." But it does suggest that being human is after all what God intended for me.

This attempt is the profound quest of a pilgrim — tentative, fluid, moving, with nothing except hope. The dialogue goes on, and in the dialogue lies our hope for a theology "big enough" for a day of change. This theology of relationship is important in a world that has to discover the joy of ready love expressed toward all men, everywhere. If, along the way, we forget who we are and where we have come from, we shall lose any grasp of love's eternal thread, for in what we have been and in what we are, lies the essence of what we shall be. *Empathy* with others who struggle, person against person, is the root of understanding that can lead to this theology of relationship. Indeed, God *is* love.

PART II
The Human Relations
Skill and Theory

5. THE TUG-OF-WAR:
TRUST OR CONTROL

Fifteen persons sit apprehensively in a circle looking at the floor, or thereabouts. They have come from four different church communities to share in a forty-eight-hour group experience advertised as a "Human Relations Lab." There are two professional leaders, who call themselves "trainers," serving as conveners of the group. Only a few participants have ever met before. One can almost read the questions each is asking mentally: Who are these people? Why did they come here? What is going to happen — to me — this weekend? Do these people know anything about me? Can I *trust* them? The battle is on: a tug-of-war between trust and our need to control.

There is a little banter, some greetings, and the request for each person to write his name on a card — the name he wants the rest of the group to use for him during the weekend. Each one pins on his name card.

One of the leaders says, "Let's get acquainted with each other by becoming aware of each other's name. Will each of you, one at a time, go to the newsprint and write your full name in large letters? Tell us about your name as you write." One by one, the members of the group complied. For some, it was an easy task. For others, more shy, it was difficult. As each finished, the group vocalized the name three or four times. A new pride in one's name developed as each person heard his name called out. There was also some name-learning by the group.

The leader continued, "On the basis of what you have learned about each other during this hour, pair off now by selecting a person in the group who you feel is most like yourself. Get to know each other a little better. I'll call you back in six minutes to report on what you've found out." Time passes. There is a lot of buzzing. Some movement.

When time is called, the members share discoveries. They find that they have spent the majority of the time talking *about* one another, but not really meeting one another. They know a lot *about* each other's past, but know little *of* each one as he is here and now.

"Let's change our tactics some," one of the trainers suggested. "With the same partner, spend the next eight minutes discussing the event (or events) that has most influenced your life until now. In fact, talk about that which has made you what you are more than anything else in the world."

Movement. Buzzing. Encounter.

When the group came back together, there seemed to be a vibrant overtone of excitement. They were breaking through the traditional "Let me tell you about myself" to a new "Let me let you know me." There was a genuine acknowledgement that, as a group, they had much in common as well as much that was excitingly different.

The group moved through one or two more action-parable experiences, shared their learnings, and then spent an exhilarating two hours defining their own personal learning goals (see chapter 2) and developing a covenant (contractual) community, with norms and guidelines that grew out of the group experience. In this interaction the whole question of trust was specifically verbalized. "Can I really trust another fellow human being with my life?" All that had happened in the three hours was only preparation for the raising of this and other vital questions. The initial answers reflected an uncertainty that words could not easily dissipate.

Our need to control is strong. It seems to be primary if we are to survive. We say: "I can trust those who prove themselves trustworthy. But that takes time. You have to know the person."

Is that trust? "If you love those who love you, what reward have you? Do not even the tax collectors do the same?" (Matthew 5: 46-47).

This concept of trust is one of the most controversial aspects of the world of the behavioral scientist. And yet, there is nothing in this sphere of human relationship that is more supported by the Christian faith than the principle that the ground of all life is *trust,* not *control.*

Do I really trust? This is also the most serious question raised in the whole sphere of experiential education. I am not referring to trust as a naive, blind folly. I am not talking about a calculated, controlling "trust." I am talking about risk and uncertainty; an adventuresome trust, reflected in the action of an Abram, a Jacob, a Jeremiah, a Jesus. I am discussing the fundamental factor of the highest of all arts, the art of loving — a high level of trust.

How is trust compatible with prior claims that discipline is basic to spontaneity, and self-control is the key to self-development? Does this conclusion not imply "control"?

The answer lies not in the way these principles are formulated, but in the very meaning of the word TRUST. Words like trust, love, hope, are actualizing words. Their real meaning is found only when an *ing* is added to them: trust*ing*, lov*ing*, hop*ing*. They are action words that reflect the being and doing of the actor, not that which is acted upon. Essentially this means that we do not do what so many of our culture suggest, "trust people and/or things out there." Trust comes from within. "Do I trust you?" Simply stated, the question really should be worded like this: "Do I trust myself with you?" or "Can I risk making myself available to you and others, because I know first of all who I am, where I am, and to whom I belong?"

This consideration makes a new examination of the essentials of trust necessary. To trust because that which is "out there" has earned our trust is to play a game of calculated risk. This is not trust, for it is less than interpersonal. It is functional and generally reflected in numerous reservations: "I will love you, if —"

We often talk of a good commitment, but when we are faced with action, once again we find the many "ifs" that condition our commitment. One group participant, finding herself caught up in a new local movement of some intensity, in a personal letter wrote:

> I am learning that the totally committed person operates in a manner that is so foreign to me I often can't recognize a political move when I'm directly in the middle of it. We, who for 2000 years in the church have talked about commitment, don't have the foggiest notion of how it operates.

This person was trying to indicate the totality of commitment — its effect on every aspect of a person's life. Such totality requires a trust that is more open than the trust we have known. What such a person is saying is: "I trust those I know will not hurt me, use me, or violate me." Parenthetically, he is saying, "And if they do hurt, use, or violate me, I will no longer trust them." This is control, not trust. Trust is *not* "out there."

Refresh your memory about the accounts of the trust encounters in the Christian tradition: Abram's call to go into an unknown country; Jacob's anxiety in relation to his brother (and even the evidence of continued fear after his wrestling with the faceless angel); the self-pity of Elijah in moments of apparent terror when he felt alone; the hostile preachments of Amos, who, out of his own poverty, threw arrows at the affluent; the terrible hurt of Jeremiah, who found hope for a new life in the midst of despair; the brash arrogance of Peter, who was still to be used of God after his denial; the compulsive and bold actions of Paul, who helped establish the early Western church; the determination of Athanasius, who pitted a living doctrine against Gnostic doctrine, was banished, returned, exiled, returned, tried again; the sensuous Augustine; the hostile Luther; the arrogant Judson; and diseased Kagawa. They all faced encounters in trust. Wherein lies this trust? WITHIN! Had Jesus waited for those "out there" to earn his trust, he would never have had the experience of the cross. He would have lived in monastic isolation. He would have remained hidden within the anonymity of his carpenter shop.

Trust lies within the man who has found a meaningful balance between his need for security and his need for creative tension. The balance always gives the edge to the creative tension. (Read Hebrews 11.)

Take a look at the life of Jesus. Each encounter held the reality of his trust in balance: with friend, with foe, with disciple, with priest, with lawyer, with Samaritan, with tax collector, with publican, with Peter, with Pilate. Trusting is like experiencing the exciting act of a trapeze artist. He mounts the high bar with practiced ease and grasps the bar that is hooked before him. The drums roll, slowly, softly, at first. Then, as he swings back and forth, the hum of the crowd indicates a mounting tension; louder and more excited roll the drums, until, with disciplined timing of a well-practiced artist, the acrobat lets go, and, hopefully, catches his partner, who, with equally good timing, has readied himself for the catch. Then, it's over. But there were moments of high risk, when he had to let go and trust both his skill and his partner's good timing.

Let me interpret this illustration for a moment. Each of us hopes to do his "own thing." Education, practice, moral values, and physical development are all a part of readying the self for that moment of letting go. The preparation creates its own tension. For some, the swing out over empty space first occurs at the age of six or seven. For others, at twelve or thirteen. For most, it comes at seventeen, eighteen, or nineteen. For a few, it comes even later. For some, it never comes. While we do our swinging, others watch, expectantly.

The tragedy of many is that they simply swing out and in, out and in. They never let go. Those who watch soon become disinterested. Too content with the security of what they know is safe, they dare not let go. Who will catch them? What if they miss? What will happen if they fall? Is that net (society) safe? Will they be helped up again? The drums grow dull, less expectant. Now and then there is a spurt of life that looks like it might happen. Then they catch themselves, and the movement of renewed excitement dies away.

For a few, those who are willing to risk, there is the thrill of letting go. At first, they play it straight. Letting go. Nothing spectacular. They get the feel of what it's like to trust, to be caught. "There! I'm safe. I'll try again. And again. A miss! Caught by the net. That's safe. Let's try it again. Something more dramatic, more adventuresome, more exciting. There, I've got it. My partner has his timing down. Take away the nets." (Now and then, there is a daring one who risks everything.) The crowd waits. The tension is high. Others may help the spirit by adding rhythm (community). Most just wait and watch — spectators. Then it happens: a Kagawa, a Livingstone, a Gandhi, a King. But there are times when they miss, and they fall to their death. A shot rings out from the crowd in the back alley, the act of a sadistic murderer-assassin.

But to let go is TRUST in the face of risk.

Trust is not swinging out and in on the glory of the past. It is not living for the future. It is doing our own thing. HERE! NOW!

We do not find it easy to contemplate personal commitment. It is easier to see commitment in historic or millennial terms. Then we don't have to trust NOW. Jesus said, "Take up the cross," NOW. "Follow me," NOW. "Come," NOW. "Behold, the kingdom of God IS IN THE MIDST OF YOU," NOW! "TODAY, this Scripture is fulfilled in your hearing." "INASMUCH AS YOU HAVE DONE IT UNTO ONE of the least of these my brethren . . ." NOW.

Trust is not a parlor game. It is spontaneous, immediate, disciplined, and tension producing. When the minister meets with his youth, regardless of the time, it is for real! When a husband meets his wife, it is for real! When the laity encounters the clergy, when a child reaches for his parents, when the poor cry out to the rich, when the black encounter the white, it is for real. And there are no gaps, except a trust gap.

This kind of trust is fundamental to experiential education and a theology of relationship. It is the ground of all loving. To trust less than this is to be the servant of fear. "God help me — I am afraid."

Look at the course of experiential learning again, as indicated in an earlier chapter.

	CYCLE I	CYCLE II
The Faith Statement:	"God is not."	"God is."
The Assumption:	Mistrust "I am afraid."	Trust "I am loved."
The Expectation:	Win/Lose "I will be hurt."	Win/Win "Shared quest."
The Experience:	Defensiveness — Control — Aggressiveness — Withdrawal	Openness — Trust — Shared responsibility — Encounter
The Reinforcement:	Destructive	Constructive
The Resolve:	Self-survival	Multiple resolution

When once a cycle is finished, it repeats itself, over and over. For most, life begins with the assumption of mistrust (Cycle I), born in fear. Regardless of his verbal acclamation of God, a man's behavior is more readily the measure of his ability to trust. The task of the prophet/church is to risk its life, in love (Cycle II), to cut through the whirl of Cycle I to bring hope.

The fearful are boxed in by their fears. The inference generally is the expectations of "others have me trapped." "THEY box me in." This is both right and wrong. The expectations (the shoulds) of others can box in a man. When we are children (from infancy to age six), we learn ways in which we can satisfactorily cope with the demands, restraints, and expectations of the adult world. We "box in" our feelings and expressions in order to get along. We are taught often that to "win" the love of the parent or guardian, we

DIAGRAM A

CYCLE I

CYCLE II

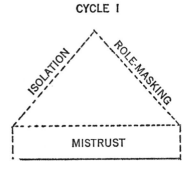

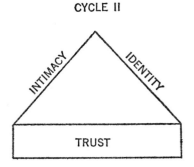

"There is no God!"	"God is."
I am afraid!	I am loved!
Separation (sin)	**Togetherness (reconciliation)**
The illusion of "being" through functional role development.	The reality of "being" through interpersonal relationships, tried and tested, and functional role development.
Alternatives: impulsive/compulsive behavior reflected in temporary addictive action (escapes). Neurotic.	**Alternatives:** spontaneity/creative innovation. Free from addictive controls. Aware of neurotic tendencies. Open to correction through feedback. Willing to risk pain.
Resolve: Everything is temporary. The more he seeks his salvation, the more he is "lost." He is boxed in.	**Resolve:** An exciting pilgrimage in which many mileposts mark the way for others. Free to be in community with others, even those who are different.

must behave "as expected." As we mature physically, intellectually, and socially, we drag the emotional "box" with us. Internally, our need to survive keeps reminding us, "This is the way to get along." Infancy. Puberty. Adolescence. Adulthood. Everything changes — except the box. Emotionally we remain fixed in an infantile or childhood world.

Why?

The person we actually are, the world we live in, the people we relate to, the games we play, the work we do — are all new, free from the encumbrances of our childhood years. That is, "new" if we have ever looked out from behind the blinders of the "should" box.

Fear or anxiety keeps us "locked in" to what we refer to as "our box." "If the expectations of others has me boxed in, why is it so? Of what am I afraid?" We are afraid of new situations, of meeting new circumstances.

The "boxed in" person is his own worst enemy. He is restricted (consciously or, more seriously, unconsciously) by his own past, again the most unmanageable part of his life. After all, who among us can change his past now? Who really wants to! This is not even the intent of analysis. Analysis is not therapy. It is only the development of grist from which understanding comes as one seeks healing. The "free" person on the other hand does not deny the expectations of others. He takes them into account. *But he decides for himself what is valid for him.* His decision does not leave him riddled with an unreal guilt. He literally takes charge of his own life.

Those who live in fear must live by control. They cannot love. They may function as if they love and call it love. They may even look like they love, but they do not love. And when a crisis comes (i.e., death, disruption of the routine), it is then that the truth of one's trust becomes known.

There are four basic needs to which men address themselves: the need for security ("I am safe"), the need for response ("I am heard"), the need for recognition ("I count"), and the need for new adventure ("I am free"). We find that the first and the last come continually into serious conflict. The choice as to which has the edge over the other will determine the satisfaction of the second and third. We need to learn how to live with that tension. Those who trust, the Abrams, Moseses, Jacobs, Jeremiahs, Pauls, Augustines, Kagawas, chose the new adventure. From their decisions came a new faith, new nation, and new worlds. From Jesus came a new commandment: "Love . . . as I have loved you" (John 15:12). Now, there is a risk!

Draw your lifeline: any line that will represent your life from beginning to end. Make it whirling, jagged, straight, curved, downward, upward; however you visualize your life. Some lines will look like those in Diagram B.

As in Diagram C, write "key word phrases" on the line to note the highs and lows, the plateaus, and what they mean in your life. Put a check mark on the line that indicates where you feel that you are "right now."

DIAGRAM B

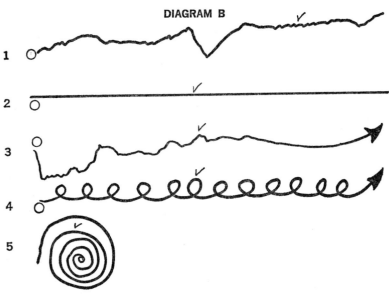

DIAGRAM C

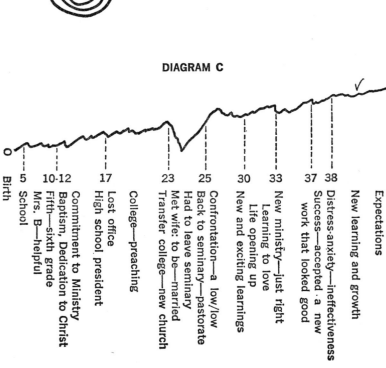

Birth

5 School

10-12 Mrs. B—helpful
Fifth—sixth grade
Baptism, Dedication to Christ
Commitment to Ministry

17 Lost office
High school president

College—preaching

23 Transfer college—new church
Met wife; to be—married
Had to leave seminary
Back to seminary—pastorate

25 Confrontation—a low/low

30 New and exciting learnings
Life opening up

33 Learning to love
New ministry—just right
work that looked good

37 38 Success—accepted a new
Distress-anxiety—ineffectiveness

New learning and growth

Expectations

Where did you put your check mark? At the end of your line? (Then you must expect to die immediately.) What does your life-line look like? Some are flat, chronological, dull, and uninteresting. Others show marks of disturbance, disruption, and tragedy. Some show growth through depth. Some just go along, upward, without any depth. Some show cycles. What does your line show? Share it with others. What does it look like to the other person?

Is the check mark where you can see the full chronological extension of your life? Have you placed the past in a too significant role so that it takes up the whole line, leaving little for the future? Why not look at your life in terms of the future? After all, there is much more that is manageable in the future than in the past. That's where TRUST really comes in. It does not take much trust to believe in what has been. Trust comes in things "hoped for." (See Hebrews 11:1.)

Can we trust in the present? Do we have the courage to let go? Or are we afraid that whatever comes will hurt too much? If we don't want to get hurt, we don't love. How often people avoid the possibility of creative resolve in their marriages, in their careers, in their social life — because it may hurt too much. Pain is not evil — unless it is consciously and sadistically inflicted. Pain is a signal. Something has gone wrong. Something is in need of repair. Hear it. All suffering, when it takes on meaning (and love brings meaning to all things), ceases to be suffering. It then becomes sacrifice. There *is* meaning in sacrifice. "I will risk being hurt if from that hurt can come reconciliation and love." This has been the overwhelming motivation of many men and women who have died in the mission service, in war, or for some other exploratory cause.

The seeker then yields the controls of life to trust. He is free to be. And so is everyone else who comes in contact with him. Anxiety is diminished. The key *is* TRUST. Its polarity is CONTROL. If trust is the key to freedom — essential to learning; then control is the non-key, resulting in more anxiety, tightened defenses, and limited learning. When anxiety increases, learning decreases.

If TRUST is the most vital consideration of any book on experiential education, then CONTROL is the most controversial consideration. (The word "CONTROL" here does not mean self-control or personal discipline. Here it means determining for others the who, when, where, and how of their lives in hope of building avenues of escape or achievement for self.)

When one begins with fear, there is another dynamic at work. Self-preservation is all important. Because we are anxious, institutions, traditions, rituals, and forms are manipulated to shore up what appears to be uncertain. This means building in external CONTROLS, substitutes for self-discipline. (The word MANIPULATE here is used in a strong negative sense. It infers exploitation and the use of others for one's own ends. The word STRUCTURE is used to refer to conditions that are structured to enable others to help themselves to be themselves.)

Few persons have not, from time to time, used some substitutes; either out of desperation, exhaustion, or as a deliberate diversion, to shore up their uncertainty. Neurotic behavior enables us to cope in a neurotic world. But these neurotic patterns may take hold of us so that they no longer serve us, but we serve them (i.e., compulsiveness, impulsiveness).

This kind of external control is related to the whole question of man's struggle with authority. Who or what is my authority? The gospel points in the direction of the individual: under God, "I am my own authority. I am responsible for my life, my actions. I must control myself."

People can place argument after argument over against that statement. "What about the care and preservation of the society? Isn't the community more important than the individual?" Basic to any relational theology is the relationship of man and his society. In fact, man and his society ARE ONE. Ideally, if every man accepts the full responsibility for himself, then society needs no further rule. Simply stated, those who live by love live above the law, and they need no reminder of their role in their chosen community.

But this is utopianism. We must live *under* the law because we have not yet found it possible to live *in* love. The law is an external CONTROL.

Unfortunately, the law does exist. It was the policy of yesterday. It leaves us with the trappings of yesterday's needs, which become so inadequate for our today encounters. Love is more immediate; more today. The law is past. It is meant as judgment. Paul said it clearly:

> He who through faith is righteous shall live. . . . When you judge another; . . . in passing judgment upon him you condemn yourself, because you, the judge, are doing the very same things. We know that the judgment of God rightly falls upon those who do such things. . . . But now the righteous-

ness of God has been manifested apart from law, although the law and the prophets bear witness to it, the righteousness of God through faith in Jesus Christ for all who believe. For there is no distinction; since all have sinned and fall short of the glory of God, they are justified by his grace as a gift. . . . I can will what is right, but I cannot do it. For I do not do the good I want, but the evil I do not want is what I do. . . . There is therefore now no condemnation for those who are in Christ Jesus. . . . We who are strong ought to bear with the failings of the weak . . . (Romans 1:17; 2:1-2; 3:21-24; 7:18-19; 8:1; 15:1).

His message to the church in Rome was basically a request for the Christian to judge no one, for judgment leads to condemnation, and condemnation leads to death. In Christ is the promise of life. Live in that love, and when others need you, help them live in it too. For Paul, the law was for those who knew nothing of the internal joy of love's own discipline. The unredeemed require the restraints of external controls. In love's light, those who have erred do seek a new kind of "answer," a release from their error, forgiveness. They hope for reconciliation and reinstatement in the community of the concerned. They are met as God's children, not as violators of the law. The temple leaders brought Mary, of the streets, to Jesus for his judgment under the law. He refused judgment.

"Never mind what the law says," said Jesus. "The law I respect, and do not violate. But this woman I love. And love is the only power I know that will make people whole and make relationships right again. That rightness she cannot earn. Perhaps what she cannot earn we can give her." And he turned to Mary, saying, "Go, and sin no more." (See John 8:1-11.)

The struggle then is between a hopeful trust that is born in love and leads to freedom and the outdated control that is born in fear and leads to condemnation.

The battle between trust and control begins early in our lives. A child is born literally "at loose ends." He spills over when he takes food in and spills over when he is ready to eliminate. He's all "oohs" and "ahs" when he should be quiet, and all tears and shrieks when he should be asleep. The adults in his world promptly set external restraints upon him in the hope of bringing him "under control." He must conform to their givens for *their* convenience.

Is that bad?

No, not all together! The real question is: how are these restraints developed? Why are they used? What is used? What parent have you known (or perhaps you are that parent yourself) who has pushed a pacifier into the child's mouth just so he will not have to listen to the child whine? It isn't too difficult to discover why it was done. It was done less to appease the child than to rid the parent of the discomfort of the child's whining. Do you think that child gets any message from the parent? What is the parent communicating to the child by such an action?

Try an action parable. (Take the time to put the book down and try it.) Put your arms in the position you would take to hold a small infant. Use your imagination. Picture an infant, newborn, lying there in your arms. You have just completed an exciting conversation in which you have been given some news about a promotion, a raise, or an award soon to be yours. You are excited. What kind of message is the baby getting? (Pause.) None? Try again! Imagine that you have just come from a very peaceful experience. Perhaps you have just had a satisfying swim, a bath, or some quiet sleep. Or felt the effect of discovering that someone important to you really cared. What kind of message does the baby get now? (Pause.) Imagine now that you have just had a fight with your spouse, your boss, or your best friend. "Beloved, my foot! She's (he's) a witch (cad). I wish I had never met her (him)." Hold the baby. What kind of message is that child getting now? (Pause.)

The lessons an infant learns through these concrete touch intonations are much more lasting and have a much greater effect upon him than all the words we speak after he is six. When Coleen runs up to Daddy and puts her arms around his legs saying, "Daddy, I love you!" Daddy responds as if he has been inconvenienced, saying (while he pushes her away), "Yes, dear, and I love you, too. But I'm too busy now!" The abstract notion of love, when this is continually reinforced by the same behavior, will have as a concomitant for years to come: "Yes . . . but I'm busy right now." Coleen may never learn that love is something more than that. The child who comes to the parent saying, "I love you," and finds at the same time a warm acceptance will later find it equally hard to permit even the worst of a single traumatic rejection to shake him from his conviction that he is loved. The images and abstractions we hold, in whatever system, are filled with the meanings that come from our own concrete experiences. The most important are the initial (or first) experiences of our infant and early childhood days. (Test that out with your feelings about school, your job, your marriage, your love, your feelings about children, etc. It takes a traumatic or a strongly self-determined event to make those first images change.)

The questions regarding control then are HOW? WHY? and WHAT? Controls motivated by the desire to protect the person from harming himself (or others) make sense. As this protective motivational factor moves along with the person's growth, the parent and/or guardians let go little by little, until the more adult controls are developed from within. As maturity arrives, the individual takes charge of his own life. That's one kind of control. It is internal. It is real discipline. But controls that are motivated by the desire to be convenienced as an adult are manipulative and really help the controlled person little toward developing his inner controls. In fact, these sharp external controls tend to restrict the person or force him to resort to severe rebellious behavior leading to chaos. The responsibility for learning, you will recall, is with the learner. The action parable is valuable in that it creates an experience that can be traumatic enough to shake loose the old walls of our "boxes," and bring into focus new worlds of personal potential that lie beyond the established walls. Jesus promised this same sense of freedom beyond the walls (law) to all who followed him; who trusted enough to love and risk.

The mismotivated control mind-set locks people in. There is no room for experimentation. There is little real learning, only imitation. Worst of all, there is no risk of failure. When a man cannot risk failure, he is not a man. He is not free. He cannot learn. To let loose of these limiting bonds, the adolescent (tragically some begin when they are older) rebels against his adult "controllers." This is a redemptive act. It is an effort to discover who he is and who he is not. He wants and needs to become his OWN AUTHORITY. A few adolescents persist long enough to find the answers. Most compromise or acquiesce too early in order to lessen the pain of separation and appease the appetite for success. "If you do it my way, I'll love you." Or "Do as I say and I'll pay you more!"

Slam! The lid is on and the box is closed. Then events and situations change all around us. Even the people who influence us change. Our own skills and knowledge change. But we remain emotionally fixed. Boxed in!

Experiential education is not a philosophy of education that external controllers will adopt. They may play the experiential education "games," but they are hardly serious about it. More often, they tend to throw up a smoke screen of suspicion and accusation. The process is labeled "demonic."

Go back to your lifeline. Think (or discuss) what you have recorded there in light of this new information. Are you free to make decisions? Do you make them? Who controls you? Who do you control? How? Do you trust? Or are you one who really needs to control? Be controlled? Can we test the control levels of a person, of a group?

There is a simple action parable that can be used for this purpose. The least threatening and the most fun is the action parable simply known as the "ball throw." Have the group move into a circle, standing. Toss in an imaginary ball (any size, shape, etc.). The directions should be clear but not too detailed. "Here, catch! This is an imaginary ball. You can play with it any way you want to. It can become any type or size ball you want it to be when it is your turn to catch and throw it. Toss it around for a few minutes. This is a nonverbal exercise."

Then, ask yourself these questions as you observe:

Who gets the ball most?

Who throws the ball to whom?

Who is innovative?

Who is ready to respond to the game suggested by another for a time, so as to get some team play going?

Does anyone play a game that involves two or three in a given action (i.e., football)?

Is it all individualized? Are the players inhibited?

Who does not play the game? Why not?

Does anyone catch the ball and pocket it? Swallow it? Destroy it?

Can they have fun? Do they lose the ball and chase it?

Does anyone "hog" the ball?

Is anyone left out?

Who are the leaders?

When the five minutes of interaction are ended, ask the group to sit down right where they are and discuss what happened. Let them make their own judgments about how they worked together, who controlled, and who saw the action as a team project rather than an individual show. Where does the individual see himself in the group?

If you want to test out the leadership in a group even more firmly, or to help a group member become aware of some leadership problems that keep the group from moving because of leadership claims by several strong, competitive, controlling persons, then try the action parable, "pick a spot."

Ask the group to stand in a circle with their elbows interlocked. Each one in the group is to select silently a spot in the room, and for sixty seconds concentrate on that spot. "Now, without saying a word, take the group to that spot."

You can imagine what takes place! Each has his own idea about where that group is going to go. And unless they can work out some nonverbal communication that will let them in on what everyone else wants, and unless they can decide cooperatively to go to every other spot in the hope of getting to one's own spot, there is a real tug-of-war.

Who pulls whom?

Who seems to be the most determined?

What is happening?

On some occasions, when the physical process is applied, new leadership comes to light. Feelings are revealed you didn't even know were there. This should not be strange. Many people do not compete verbally.

After five minutes, ask the group to sit down and discuss what they just witnessed. Stay *here* and *now*. The conversation should be lively. Relate the experience to what was going on earlier in the group. How can we help persons who come to every meeting with their own idea of where the group should go? Is it important to have each person feel a sense of personal achievement in the group interaction?

For the most part, a discussion based on trust and control is very threatening to men and women who have spent their lives functionally striving for control. For them, control of persons and the environment have been very important survival concerns. There are many ways to control. One group participant, Mike, controlled his fellow workmen by withdrawing; often with the suggestion that he knew something about them that they didn't want him to know. Never sure that he didn't know something about them, they held their distance. They felt hostile and manipulated. Angela discovered that she could move in fast on a group and, through her bizarre manner and aggressive acts, take over the whole group process, guaranteeing herself a place of importance. If anyone opposed her, it was not long before that person was either out of the group or terribly uncomfortable within the group. Sue discovered that she had a magnetic effect upon some group people, especially upon overprotective men. All she had to do was feign some hurt, and she had several running to her aid. Don would enter every argument. When things got a little tough, he would pull out his authoritative "text" and let fly with, "Well, it says here. . . ."

To combat the ugly forces of control, one generally uses the rule of thumb that suggests a viable mutuality: *If you want to influence me, then I need to know that I can influence you.* This is an antidote for control. Mutuality is the first obvious action that reflects the trust essential to our relationships. It indicates that there is rapport, an openness, and an acceptance on both sides. Control is just the opposite. It is individualized defensiveness. It is not mutual. It is closed. Sometimes it shows through subtleties: puns, humor, hurts, moods, words, and rules. At other times, it comes through more directly as rejection, hostility, pity, and sentimentality. Either way, control is alienating. Mutuality, the beginning of trust behavior, is reconciling. It suggests a growing maturity.

What do I mean by *maturity?* When we are children, beginning in the very first moments of our life, we are involuntarily dependent. We need our parents (or whatever substitutes for parents there may be). But from that day, our will to be a free agent is taking on a shape of its own. As the child reaches the age of six, seven, or sometimes eight, the old involuntary dependence begins to give way so that the child can move about freely; at first, in his own world of fantasy. As he matures, he asserts his uniqueness even more, moving out of fantasy (hopefully) into reality. This move often brings him into conflict with his parents or guardians. In effect, his adolescent years are spent trying to get the message across to his elders that he is his "own man."

To some adults the message comes hard. Again, there is not a generation gap, but a trust gap. The parent responds to the new adult out of fear: "I must control him. He may hurt himself. He may separate himself from me. Then I will be hurt." Trust is questioned. Communication breaks down. Separation is caused by the very act that one has performed in the hope of not being separated. Jesus said that he who seeks to save his life will lose it. He who loses his life, for my sake (for love's sake), will find it. (See John 12:25.)

We need to remember that this adolescent outburst is necessary.

It even needs to be encouraged by knowing adults. Tragically the outburst may be stifled and comes out when a person reaches forty or fifty, only to affect many others whom he would rather not hurt, such as spouse or children.

When maturity does come, it brings with it several realizations:

1. *I am dependent,* therefore I will choose wisely my dependencies, spouse, work, values, institutions, etc.
2. *I must trust others for my own well-being* because community is essential to life.
3. *All judgment is projection* which is self-revealing and self-exposing. I can see only in others what I know to be in me.
4. *If life is to be exciting, I cannot play it safe.* There is risk in all adventure.
5. *I will be my own man and not a scapegoat* by blaming others when I have learned to trust, and to trust again and again.

The mature mind hears the words of Jesus and reads them as relevant: "Be not anxious." "Fear not." "Be not afraid." The ground of the mature man is TRUST. It is this trust that leads to salvation, not control. And salvation is only found in RELATIONSHIP.

Mutuality is an eye-level experience. What this means is that in every encounter I must know that I have the right and responsibility to control me, and only me. I must give to all others a similar right and responsibility. Regardless of content, the contact must affirm this mutual respect. Anything less than this is condescension and/or subservience.

You can test this out by asking yourself: In my personal relationships, in group life, in my work, how are decisions made? By whom? What role do I play in the decision making?

Are they made by a minority? Minority control is the control of a few who tend to dominate by sheer will and force (verbal, intellectual, or physical). This leaves a number of people unhappy, as they concur to the will of a few under duress. Are there decisions made by a majority or by default? Majority control is certainly more democratic. It at least appears to be "fair" for the larger number of persons. Of course, when one hundred vote and a majority of fifty-one wins, a lot of discontented people are still left. Are decisions made by consensus? Consensus is the style of group control that permits an accounting of and for every person in the community. It permits mutuality in every encounter. A group member is not coerced, cajoled, or manipulated into "harmonizing."

The process may take longer initially. But it brings everyone to a position more satisfying to interpersonal relationships, and certainly more ready for commitment.

To test this out, use the "bomb shelter" action parable. "You are one of seven persons in a bomb shelter; a shelter which holds only ten persons, with provisions for the two-week 'all clear' period declared essential in the event of a nuclear attack. Word has come that there is a nuclear missile en route to the area and you have secured yourselves in this shelter. There are nine people outside the door, hoping to get in. They are: a young pregnant woman; her husband (a bookkeeper); an armed police officer; a professional athlete; a fifty-year-old Franciscan priest; a young, wealthy co-ed; a famous musician; a Negro second-year medical student; an astronomer (male). You can only take three of those persons. Which three will you allow to come in?"

After the group has worked toward a decision for fifteen minutes, note the results and then raise the following questions:

Were you listened to? How do you feel about how you influenced the decision?

Who seemed to be the most helpful in the process?

What blocked group movement?

How did you make the selection? Was the process satisfactory?

What would you change in the process next time?

Will you trust this group to make an important decision for you? Why? Why not?

There is a fine line between control and mutuality especially in decision making. And that line is often evaluated through the motive of the participant:

CONTROL — Am I using this person for my own good? Am I helping in the hope of controlling? Can I risk exposure, or do I need to control for the sake of my image?

MUTUALITY — Am I involved as an enabler in the hope that the other may become more truly himself, irrespective of me? Can I really level? Can I expose myself? Am I open?

Jesus was a mutual person. What he claimed for himself he claimed for all mankind. "I lay down my life. . . . No one takes it from me, but I lay it down of my own accord. I have power to lay it down, and I have power to take it again" (John 10:17-18).

Paul described this action to the church at Philippi: "he . . . emptied himself" (Philippians 2:7a).

6. QUESTIONS OF INCLUSION

"Where do I fit in? Am I a part of this group (family, team, staff, task force)? For what do I count? Who cares? Can I change my role and be accepted? Will someone notice? Is it desirable? Where do I fit in?"

Have you ever asked yourself these questions? Have you heard others ask them — verbally or nonverbally? Why does anyone ask them?

Who one is (identity) is strongly related to *where one belongs* and *to whom one is related* (intimacy). These personal factors are essential for a person's sense of well-being. I am free to be only when I know WHO I AM and TO WHOM (or to what group, family, team, etc.) I BELONG. These personal factors, then, are tied up with the whole approach of the experiential educator.

Experience-based education requires a full participation in group life and learning by the learner as well as the teacher-learner. Spectator education, more popularly known as monological lecturing (the lecture can be dialogical), is less effective. To "learn about" life is a passive investment. There is little risk to reading, hearing, and viewing on a screen (except to the most imaginative who may either take flight in their fantasies or find themselves motivated to get more involved). To learn life is an active process, demanding greater risks.

Every person needs the assurance in an educational laboratory experience that he can risk; that the variables will be so limited that he can learn from the experiences rather than be frightened further by them. With some trust, the learner moves out to meet the unknown in a community of trusted peers. There, four basic factors must be visible:

1. *My personhood will be preserved.*

Who I am and what I am, though I will be encountered, will be respected at all times. I will feel a reasonable sense of quiet confidence in this situation and with this group of people. I will be in control of what I do. I will be in control of what others are able to do with and to me. I am responsible.

2. *I feel that I belong.*

I feel that I am needed in this group. My feelings and thoughts are listened to. Response does come. I contribute to the emerging life of the group and feel both appreciated and appreciative.

3. *The community is important to me.*

I feel responsible for the ongoing life and meaning of the group. Everything that happens is my concern; indirectly sometimes, directly at other times. I must be present at all times. I must be aware of the goals and norms of the group. I must work for a cohesion based more on understanding than on agreement.

4. *I need to be understood and to understand.*

The greatest gift of community at its best is the gift of understanding. The individual needs to feel that he is known for who and what he really is, not for what he can do or say. Such understanding permits the further expansion of his openness until his life fully blooms. This self-acceptance and other-acceptance is part of the mutuality suggested before as imperative to the love relationship. It is the ground for empathy, compassion's heart and soul.

These personal factors can so free the learner that he can build new images and experiences without the threat of being wiped out, caught up, or trapped in a maze of human exploitation. In this world, he is free to experiment: win or lose.

But these factors are not readily available in most of our groupings. We are too easily threatened when: (1) the persons we are to encounter have different standards of living than we do; (2) we are pressured to conform; (3) we find it difficult to verbalize how and what we are feeling, or what happened; (4) our conscience and moral values become rigid, inflexible; (5) we cannot climb over our stored reservoirs of guilt, hostility, and/or sentiment which we have repressed; (6) our own personal ambitions are frustrated; and/or (7) we feel that we are being exploited without our own consent.

These factors are all important in considering the structural development of a contract or covenant arrangement. Adherence lends itself to coherence.

The group's inclusiveness can be tested out in several ways: How do we relate to one another in this group? Use a sociogram as an action parable. It is easily drawn by the participants. The following instructions can be used:

> Draw a large circle in the middle of your paper. Let the large circle represent the space that we can define as our group space. Find a spot in that space where you feel you belong. Draw a small circle and put your initials in it. If you believe that you are not in the group, put your circle outside of the large circle. Initial it.
>
> Now draw a small circle for every other member of the group, and put their initials in their circle. Be sure to space the circles in such a way so as to demonstrate to the group how you feel they relate to you and to the group as a whole. Take five or six minutes.

When everyone has completed his diagram, ask the members of the group to pass the pictures around the group. Have each person note in regard to each picture:

> Where did this person place himself?
> Where did he place me?
> What does the group look like from this person's point of view? Is his picture like my point of view? Why? Why not?
> Does it make sense?

In examining the circle, note the following:

> Is there a circle for everyone? Who is missing?
> Who seems to be outside the group? Does he feel in, or is he only comfortable with one or two persons?
> If he feels in, what does he or the group want to do about it?
> How are the circles arranged? Who is in the center of things? Is there agreement among the members about this?
> Who goes through others in order to feel a part of the group?
> Do any of the circles touch (interpersonal), or is it strictly a functional group, developing roles that will help them fulfill their given task?

These questions and others should be discussed thoroughly.

A second action parable is more active.

If you want the group to demonstrate for each other their feelings about their participation in the group (or their influence on the group), have them stand again in a circle. Begin the instructions by saying, "This circle represents the outer dimension of a cartwheel. Each one of you is standing on a spoke of that wheel, leading to the hub in the center. This is a wheel that will help us discover where we are as participants in this group. Those who feel that they are a real part of this group will move up their spoke toward the center of the circle. Those who feel that they are 'in' but to a lesser degree, will put themselves in where they feel most comfortable. Those who feel 'out' of the group completely will step back behind the outer dimension of the wheel. Test out the place you put yourself by moving in and out until you feel comfortable with your position in relation to the others in the circle. Do it for yourself. It is done nonverbally. Take three or four minutes."

After the group has moved in and out and taken their positions, ask them to freeze. "Now examine where you are and where everyone else is." Sit and discuss how you feel about it.

There will be a lot of interaction. If the group finds itself in a tight-knit circle, close together, then it is an unusual group. (It might be worthwhile asking this group the question: Is there room in this group for selectivity, individualization, disagreement, etc.?) Generally the persons dot the wheel at various points, indicating degrees of participation, leadership, and inclusion.

While considering the question of inclusion, you might want to measure the influence of persons in the group. "Who influences our group life the most? The least? Do you feel that one person is making more of an impact on the group than some of the others? Some have dropped out completely. Who are they?"

Another action parable may be developed in one or two ways, depending upon what you want to get from the experience. Both ways may be tried successively. The leader should be ready to work with a good deal of feeling and conflict. Begin with the general experience. "These chairs are lined up in a row, one for each person in the group. Now, take the chair you feel you should occupy according to your influence on this group. Chair number one is for the person who carries the most weight in group leadership. The last chair is for the one who feels his word carries the least weight. Test out the chair you are sitting in. If you feel you must move, you may move up or down for a few minutes. If you cannot persuade someone else in the row to give up his chair, then you may want to move your chair to the front or back of him, until it seems right. Test your position out for a few minutes. This is all nonverbal." Then freeze. Note the positions. What happened? Does the group agree with those who placed themselves high and low? What can be done, if anything needs to be done, about the ones who feel "out of it"?

The second alternative is to have one person at a time place people where he thinks they belong in the line of influence. In this experience, you will add a dimension to the above control exercise. Ask, "Who influences me personally in this group, and why?"

These are various kinds of inclusion action parables that lead persons to experience how it really seems to be with them in a group. Why should this be done at all? For two primary reasons: first, it helps the individual to make concrete what previously was only assumed — "This *is* where I belong right now"; second, it gives the person and the group the open opportunity to do something about the group relationships if he or they want to.

If you want to test out the cohesive feelings of the group, there are several action parables that can be used. The following micro-lab can be used as a two-hour experience in group cohesiveness. (A micro-lab is a life experience in miniature. Several experiences can be compressed into a two- or three-hour period in which many factors related to a human relations concern can be experienced.)

After a brief warm-up period, and having established goals and norms relevant to the object of this micro-lab experience which have culminated in a covenant-contract between the participants and the participant leaders, have the group come into a full circle. In silence, look at each participant fully and carefully (5 minutes). Discuss the feelings (5 minutes).

Instruct the participants as follows: "I'm going to call out some signals. I want you to form groups according to the number I call out. If you do not have that number of persons in your group, you will not be considered a group. Any questions?"

Rapidly, with brief pauses for interaction and to catch the feelings, call off several numbers: three, five, seven, four, six, nine, eleven. Observe what happens. Stop on occasion and ask them to internalize for a moment. (To "internalize" here means to get in touch with what you are feeling; pull the unconscious feelings to the conscious level, and hold them there. This is done individually.) "What's happening inside you right now? How do you feel about where you are and what is happening to you? Do not share it yet, but record it in your mind." Go on with three or four more sets of group exchange.

Let the group sit and internalize for two or three minutes. Then have them share their feelings. After sufficient ventilation (to "ventilate" means to express the "right now" feelings), ask the group to examine in specifics: What happened and to whom? Analyze the experience. Why did it happen this way? What were the results? Generalize about the experience. What will you do differently next time?

Now give the participants time to practice their new learnings. "For the next thirty minutes we are going to experience a verbal and nonverbal action parable. The group will be divided into separate subgroups (about five each). Each group will consider themselves a fully constituted church body, with all the rights and privileges of membership. You must develop your criteria for membership. Then, using those criteria, select one member of your subgroup to be eliminated (excommunicated). You *must* eliminate one person. You have fifteen minutes for this half of the experience."

Observe carefully as the subgroups develop their criteria. Sense some of the anxiety in all of the participants. Do not interfere with the process, but keep them on the point. They will want to digress, avoid, even balk.

When this portion of the action parable has been completed, ask them to internalize individually what they have been going through. Be sure their feelings register, but do not discuss them. "Now each of the excommunicated members is to seek membership in one of the other subgroups. Using the same criteria that each subgroup developed for membership previously, decide whether he will be received or not. Do not eliminate criteria. Those who are seeking membership should continue to seek it until they find a group that will let them in."

The action follows.

Internalize: What do you feel right now? Let these feelings register. Now discuss the whole experience.

Ventilate: How did you feel? What happened to make you feel that way?

Identify: What was happening?

Analyze: What was helpful in this experience? What was not so helpful? What were the results?

Generalize: What would you do differently next time?

In drawing out learnings, relate this experience both to the earlier nonverbal encounter and to what happens in so many churches and church groups today. What are legitimate criteria for church membership? Is the church to be inclusive? What happens when someone is rejected?

After a brief pause for informal discussion and a "break," bring the group together to discuss a third action parable. It would be helpful if two or three of the group members sat in an outer circle with the leader and observed this next experience. Our concern is for those who will be rejected and their feelings. The decision must be made by consensus.

Say to the group: "You are —— in number. You have just been shipwrecked and find yourself in the water clinging to the side of a rubber life raft that will safely hold two-thirds of you. You can only hope to survive the icy waters by getting into the life raft within ten or twelve minutes. Who will climb in and live? Who will remain in the perilous water? You have twelve minutes to decide."

Observe: By what criteria did they make the selection? Whose voice was heard most strongly? Did they feel the urgency of the situation? What behavior did you observe? Were there martyrs? Did the group make the decision or did some individuals make it?

Internalize: What are your feelings right now? Discuss them. Ventilate. Identify. Analyze. Generalize.

Dealing with people today, especially while under the pressure of survival, is no simple task. The tendency is to depreciate personhood — to make people into "things." Treating people as if they were "things" makes the supposed subject an object. When the "I" uses another as an "it," then they both become an "it." The action parable is an experience that enables the participant to practice the "I — Thou" relationship in behavior under pressure.

It is important now to develop input related to the whole question of identity and intimacy: Who am I and where do I really belong?

The next action parable is both verbal and nonverbal. Divide the group into subgroups of six. Ask one member of each subgroup to take his turn first in the center of his subgroup. Let the subgroups know that you, as the micro-lab leader, are going to ask questions of the person in the middle of the group as well as give directions to each subgroup simultaneously. The person in the center needs to concentrate on his feelings and internalize as the action parable moves along. The subgroup should follow the directions carefully without talking. Let them know that you will need the participants' full cooperation to make this happen.

Ask the subgroup members to form a circle around the main person, keeping about six or seven feet away from him. Address the respondent throughout the following procedure with the exception of the instructions you will need to give to the subgroup.

"Look fully into the face of each of these five persons, turning as you do, until you get the feel of their presence. (Pause.) How do you feel about being there in the center of things?" Internalize the feelings. Let them register. (Pause.)

"Group, turn around. (Pause. Action.) Now, how do you feel as you look at these same people?" Internalize.

"Group, move away slowly. Very slowly. One step at a time. How do you feel as you watch these people move away from you?" Internalize.

"Group, turn around and move slowly toward him. Keep moving until I tell you to stop. (Pause.) How do you feel now?" Internalize.

The group keeps moving until they have pulled tightly together with the main person locked into the center of the group. He cannot move. He is restricted. "What are your feelings now?" Internalize.

"Group, turn around and lock him in just as tightly. Now what are your feelings?" Internalize.

"Place these people where you will feel comfortable with them." Give the center person time to place each person where he wants them. Internalize.

Generally they will be placed about one to three feet away where they can easily be touched when necessary, but where the touching will not restrict the personal action desired by the main person. The group will generally be facing him. Internalize.

If you want to test out further the balance, suggest that the main person reach out and touch each person at will, and have them respond. Then ask the group to place their hands on the center person's shoulders. Press down slightly. This appears to be restrictive again, even burdensome. Internalize.

Have the center person reach up through the web of arms and take hold of two arms. His reaching up, in turn, will bring some release from the weight. It will release the pressure. Internalize.

Let every one in each subgroup experience this action before there is any discussion. Then let them sit down and share what they have felt in this experience. Listen to the feelings of: "I don't like it — it is too confining" (I want to be free); "I like it — it is warm and comfortable" (womb-like); or "I can stand it for a while." The movement to a position where there is freedom to move suggests the true style of the truly intimate. "Others are close enough to reach me and to be reached when it seems necessary, but they are far enough away so that I can be my own man and risk some things." *In intimacy, there is a closeness, and there is a distance.* A paradox, but true. Can the group develop learnings from this experience that can help them in their next intimate confrontation?

Long group discussions can follow. When are we being intimate? When are we not being intimate? When is it all right to seek to be alone? When is it necessary to be with others? One young college co-ed felt that intimacy was giving herself sexually to the fellows she dated. In therapy, she discovered that her actions were abortive attempts at intimacy. She really feared intimacy. Sexual intercourse was her way of not being intimate. A student felt that belonging was the all important thing. He sublimated his values in order to get along with more violent peers. It led him into some events that terminated in an arrest, a trial, and a subsequent imprisonment. A businessman felt that he could do everything for himself, that intimacy was "not that important," only to find himself shelved with a severe heart disease at the age of thirty-six, without family or friends. A housewife couldn't interact with her children because "they demanded too much" of her. Her time and her person were locked in by earlier obligations. In a sudden wave of bitter hostility, the marriage collapsed. All are asking the question in one way or another, What does it mean to be close?

God again gives an answer in the very paradox of his own Being: in his very nearness there is a suggested distance. It means living in the tension that exists between the fear of being close and the desperate need to be close. The alternatives to this creative tension of the intimate relationship are only two: escape or neutrality. For many in our world of apathy, it is both.

Again, the ground of this interaction is LOVE. On the one hand the beloved and on the other hand the lover are able to say, "I've got to be me," while in the same breath they are saying, "I'll help you be you." God's greatest gift is disclosed in the intimate recess of a relationship where one is affirmed.

This theology of relationship suggests that it took Jesus *and* the disciples to get the kingdom of God into being. It took a love relationship with an impetuous Peter, a wayward Mary, a learned Nicodemus, a concerned Mary (the mother of Jesus), and many others to make it all happen. Intimacy is born when and wherever adults discover that they need each other.

This kind of intimacy does not imprison. It frees. It leads us quite readily to the whole question of identity. How often married persons hold each other off because they fear that intimacy means the loss of identity, imprisonment. As one wife put it, "When I let him have some of me, he swallows me up." This is not intimacy. This is not love. This needs to be labeled for what it is: symbiosis or exploitation, based on need. It is a form of control. Intimacy does not require that one person give up his personhood for the sake of the relationship.

One way to get the group to affirm one another is to experience an "I am" encounter. Have one person lead. He moves from person to person, with the one he first touched following him in succession (one after the other). He puts his two hands on the shoulders of the next group member he is encountering, and says: "Your name is _____. I am who I am. And my name is _____." After the experience, take time to internalize it.

Discuss it. Pull learnings from it to the end that those who share in community have found both the joy of intimacy (love) and the excitement of their own individual identity (that, too, is love).

In this environment, a person is free to learn, for he is ready now to encounter other beings fearlessly.

7. TO REACT OR RESPOND

At first glance, the words REACT and RESPOND seem to imply the same thing. After all, a reaction comes *as* a response.

At the risk of making too fine a distinction, I want to suggest not only that there is a difference in the expression of REACTIONS and RESPONSES but that there is also a difference in the motivation and consequences.

To *react* is to act in reciprocity; that is, to give back "in kind" (used with the telling prepositions "on" or "upon"). Reaction is dependent upon an external stimulus "out there," and implies opposition, or the will to move so as to reverse the present movement so it will flow in the opposite direction. Reaction is more than a staying influence. It is a counterattack. It, by its very nature, implies that the source of these feelings is in hostilities or sentiments bred in the past.

To *respond* is an act of communication. The stimulus is internal, beginning not within the context of vengeance or attack, but in the context of empathy and compassion. It implies that the listener is willing to flow with the actor, though this does not mean that the listener is always saying "yes." He is not counterattacking, but working out, in a flow of concern, the concerns of the speaker. He begins in a spirit that affirms both the speaker and himself. It is both mature and mutual.

Which person are you — a reactor or a responder?

In a laboratory setting persons who have been encouraged by what appear to be new norms for group interaction, and wanting something more than the general routine of a task-oriented involvement, reach out gingerly to test the climate: "Did you really mean what you said to George? That sounded rather harsh." There is a quick flurry of apology and an embarrassment that leads to the suppression of feelings. The questioner, realizing that the climate is not right for encounter, backs off again. Their actions are like those of a little boy who wants to touch a forbidden something "out there." He waits for what he considers an advantageous time. He darts out a little and runs back in. If there is no reaction this time, he'll try again, with a little more bravery. He works at it carefully until finally he touches the untouchable and then he draws back somewhat satisfied because he defied the authorities who decree, "Don't touch!"

We have heard it said (in countless ways), "Don't rock the boat!" "Keep things impersonal!" Or better yet, "Don't get personal." The common norm for group interaction in our adult world is, "Let's agree to play each other's game. It's less embarrassing that way. You tell your lies and I'll tell mine. We know what each of us is doing. But if you don't call me on it, I won't call you on it." "Lie? I don't lie to anyone! I'm perfectly honest in my actions!" someone protests.

There is a real difference between the words HONESTY and TRUTH. Again, like the reactionary as opposed to the respondent, these words reveal both the motive and the destiny of the interactors. A man can be honest and not tell the truth, just as he can react without responding. In summary, my theory is as follows:

DIAGRAM A

Functional	Functional-Interpersonal
Reaction	Response
Hostilities	Anger
Sentimentality	Affection
Honest	Truthful
Deliberate Dealings	Spontaneous Encounter

Let me illustrate. There are three sons who have, for some years, held their parents at some distance. "It's the only way we can cope," one of the sons reported. "If we try to get too close, someone always gets hurt. Mother does not want the truth. So I'm not going to encounter her. It only hurts her. I won't lie to her. I just won't tell her all that I feel and think. What she doesn't know won't hurt her."

On the other hand, the mother, from time to time, makes overtures toward her sons and her husband in the hope that one of them will hear her cry. "I have never had a satisfying person-to-person response. I don't know what it is to respond healthily. Can anyone teach me? Even one of my sons. I am a person. I would like to know that someone is taking me seriously. Perhaps then, I can give up the struggle against my buried feelings of hostility and sentimentality, and live more in the here and now. I could become a learner, in exchange for my present need to learn about. Help me *be!*"

There is no help for her apart from the truth.

HOSTILITY — SENTIMENTALITY VS. ANGER — AFFECTION

There is, in every human being, a division of feelings. We refer to them often as negative or undesirable feelings (anger) and positive or desirable feelings (affection). In more sophisticated relationships, one does not see these polarities as negative (anger) and positive (affection) except in the sense that one defines the polarities in a battery as a "minus" and "plus." To discuss feelings and response, we must take into account both poles. Half a battery is of no use at all. Half of our feelings is of little consequence. I am now distinguishing between types of plus and minus feelings. The more positive here-and-now feelings of anger and affection are not to be construed to include hostility and sentimentality.

Why do I indicate a division of feeling between the first polarization of anger and affection and the second hostility and sentimentality? Hostility and sentimentality are "dirty feelings." That is, they come out of the past. Hostility reflects a wellspring of past angers dutifully suppressed. As indicated in an earlier chapter, the less attractive feelings, such as anger, bitterness, resentment, envy, and jealousy are refused expression in our world. They are not comfortable words. They imply a weakness, a lack of control, a vulnerability. "Don't express them. Keep them to yourself."

Consequently, the unconscious self becomes a reservoir of less pleasant feelings, while the world hears the more pleasant feelings. In time, if the reservoir becomes sufficiently crammed with angry feelings — unresolved — then someone comes along with the final "straw" (it matters little who or what it is), the fire builds up a new head of steam trapped in and already overflowing the inner cistern. It is forced to blow. (I lose my temper, go on a binge, scream and slam doors, go buy some things, get in trouble.) The individual acts out his feelings. It more rightly should be said, "reacts!" His feelings come from many sources. The spray that results is meant for nobody in particular and everyone in general. Whoever is standing there gets it. There is nothing redemptive in the action. Those involved fall into three categories: (1) *the reactor* — usually incoherent and not ready to learn new behavior, (2) *the victim* — offended, who withdraws until it is over, (3) *the observer* — helpless and vague regarding cause.

The reactor gets no real help because his readiness for learning is flung aside in moments that can be described only as convulsive. The victim gives no real help, because he reacts out of his fear neurotically by withdrawal, or more aggression, rooted in either fear or guilt. The observer, uncertain of the source of anger, stands by helplessly. The victim and observer are no more ready for learning than the reactor. Indeed, they all react to each other. It becomes a whirlpool. There can be no resolve. What follows is equally disarming. There is a period of calm that suggests the storm is over and everything is back to normal (i.e., alcoholic). And there is calm for a time, the length of which is directly related to the person's ability to hold his hostility in, as it builds up a new head of steam. Then he blows again.

Sentimentality comes from the same source — only with an artificial sweetener added. At the least provocation, tears flow. Occasions of real sorrow lead to an overreaction. Motion pictures, television, and music draw great rivers of water from within. But moments that require a genuine affectionate response leave these same persons cold and distant. They have learned to love only in fantasy. As children, their will to be affectionate was turned back on them with "Not now," "I'm busy," or "Don't be silly." They are left with too much feeling gone sour.

Response on the other hand reflects a truth that is borne out of trust. Sometimes I am angry, even hateful (full of hate). Sometimes I am affectionate, joyful (full of joy). Both are a part of my passion, essential to my being a whole (fully charged) person. Both must be expressed in the here and now, freely but not without reason.

Now many of us report our response as "I don't like what you just did. I hate that. But I love you." This statement is functionally helpful, perhaps, but it is not the truth. A trust relationship means that the person is free to say "I am angry. I hate you!" When both parties in the relationship are being adult, it simply conveys, "Right now, I am angry; and I trust you with me when I am angry." On the other hand, to be affectionate is to be equally vulnerable. "I am happy, and I trust you with my joyous feelings." This, too, can be risky. This, too, demands trust.

Love and hate are the poles of passion. The intensity of each is dependent upon our ability to be passionate. The expression of anger and affection are the behavioral expressions of passion.

How can a man feel joy and think hate at the same time? I have trouble with persons who try to make their "good" feelings (acceptable feelings) right and their "bad" feelings (taboo feelings) wrong. In feelings, there is no right and wrong. One can *feel* love only as *one* feels whatever passion is predominant *right now*. The joy of this recognition lies in three realities: (1) it is here and now; (2) it is directed toward specifics; and (3) it can be resolved.

Jesus was a man capable of passionate anger. Call it "righteous indignation"; call it whatever you want, it was still anger. At times his feelings were accompanied by some violence. It is hard to objectify that with an "up there, out there" *agapē*.

The Greek *eros, philia,* and *agapē* definition of love is no more valid for the Hebraic-Christian than is the Greek division of man: body, mind, and spirit. We cannot separate love into neat *eros, philia,* and *agapē,* and reserve the latter for our moments of high-minded splendor. Love is all of these, and more. Anything less is not love, only the figure of someone's imagination. The developmental stages may be apparent. But they must be noted on a continuum, not placed in separate bins. We slice love up in the hope of controlling it. Love is personal. The personal is the Holy Spirit in life. There can be no control — only trust. When a man claims to be free only to be "full of joy," when he cannot get angry, he is the prisoner of a lie.

Love, then, has its plusses and its minuses. Because it is popularly believed that anger is a minus, one tends to think of it this way. But a great deal of good grows out of anger, as well as from joy; as much, if not more, learning comes from pain as from pleasure.

Knowing who I am means that I know that I am sometimes

joyful and sometimes hateful; but in all things, I resolve to remain intimate (that is, together, in relationship).

How can I be joyful and hateful at the same time?

One generally is not both at the same time. Joy and hate interact, depending upon our here-and-now feelings.

To examine these feelings, use this action parable:

Close your eyes. Shut out the world around you, and fantasize with me for a moment. You are alone. You have carved out for yourself a large bubble that you can call "my space." The space in it is yours. There is plenty of room. The color reflects the color you have chosen for yourself. You are not without freedom, air, and comfort. Take the time now to internalize this.

As you consider the condition of your life-space, there is another bubble moving toward you from the right. A person, whose space is his own and whose color is his own, is approaching your space. You recognize that person as loving, tender, and warm. You are full of affection as his bubble meets yours. The two become one. You touch. You are thrilled in each other's response. He leaves. But you hold on to the feelings. You consider the feelings; list them out in front of you as if they were labels that you can tear out and paste up on the bubble wall. You sit back and look at your labeled feelings, and you find comfort in them.

Suddenly, a not-so-pleasant awareness occurs to the left of you as another bubble approaches. The person is one you would rather not meet right now. You have had some serious differences. You are angry with him. With all of this discomfort and anger, he invades your bubble. The fighting continues. As quickly as possible you dismiss him. But the feelings remain. You see them "out there," labeled. You are uncomfortable. You cut out the labels and paste them up on the left-hand side of the bubble wall, careful not to have them touch the right-hand wall. You think about both sides. That's you — both sides! You've had a glimpse inside.

Some will refuse to address the more "negative" side. It is too painful. Or they will protest, saying, "I've resolved those feelings." Or, "I don't hate anybody." This person has either defected to the gods (a "should" self-image), or he has only succeeded in sublimating the "negative" of characteristics, fearing rejection. At this point, we "out-Christ" Christ, and "out-God" God. Was it not Jesus who implied that even God knew what it meant to be wrathful? There's something phony about the "I never get angry" person.

The way a person responds to conflict often tells us where he is in his relationship to self and others. There are three fundamental styles of response:

1. Paralyzed — "I can't move."

2. Computerized — "I'll do what I've been programmed to do!"
3. Actualized — "I am free to try new ways of coping, even if it may mean failure!"

The actualized person is the only one operating from a trust level which is born in mutuality. In all encounters, individual identities are respected. Once these survival characteristics are secure, love is free to move out into the world of uniqueness and difference to bring meaning and utility to a man's life. To these free persons, to know is to be known. To be known is to know. The commonness that binds a person to a person, that cements relationship in a way that all external obstacles are as windmills, becomes apparent. That kind of love breeds both self-awareness and empathy. This sense of having much in common frees us to ask the next questions: Wherein are we different?

Those who lead from a defensive position (mistrust, therefore suspicion) operate on a different premise: "We are more different than alike. Whatever we have in common is clouded by differences." Living with this premise leads to separation, alienation (new denominations) and war (or violent dissent). Individually, it leads to divorce, psychosis, compulsiveness, alcoholism, crime, or maybe even a new "escape car."

In maturity a person assumes the full responsibility for his own actions and feelings. He is free, then, to actualize both himself and the self with others. The preparation for this kind of actualization begins early in life. We move from the dependence of early childhood through the adolescent struggle for independence to adulthood.

Adulthood means interdependence. There is a built-in flexibility (spontaneity) that meets change in persons and events without despair or hysteria. Problems are seen as "shared quests," not punishments and threats. Persons seeking this kind of maturity can find it in small covenant community groups whose criteria permit each person to respond to every other one without fear of self-annihilation. Let us consider the criteria for these groups at length:

1. *We live here and now.* The tendency for many of us is to refuse to cope with the immediate. We avoid an encounter by referring to one of two things: "things back at the office, the church, the house, the club, etc." . . . or "When my ship comes in, I'm going to. . . ." It is always safer to talk about what has been

or what is going to be. One of the thrilling aspects of the teaching-learning encounter in the church is that *it is here and now.* The action parable is one tool that helps us develop enough here-and-now data to enable the group to learn from each other. It sets in motion one of the most important principles of the whole teaching-learning process: we can learn from each other.

2. *We do not violate the confidences of others.* This is one of the hardest things we have to do as a participant. There are several TRUST principles that need to be reiterated here. Realizing that a man's own person is his alone, he must be able to share without the fear of his person being threatened. When a person begins asking me a question with "That sounds interesting, tell me more" or "I'm curious about that, tell me more," I am leary. I want to back off. Interest and curiosity are self-oriented agendas which mean: "What's in this that will excite me or give me something to talk about in another group, from the pulpit, or in a class."

On one occasion, a pastor was called to task by his fellow group members for revealing in his sermon a dialogue shared in confidence just the week before. His response was, "But I disguised it well. I didn't use any names." But the level of emotional investment held by the person it exposed was so severe that he was driven away from getting further help with his problem, at least in that setting. EXPOSURE carries with it threat enough even with one person, let alone with many. A person will think twice before he becomes open. Rob a man of his secrets and you rob him of his humanity. All sharing is confidential.

3. *We will trust each other and assume the risks for ourselves.* People are human. They do err. For this reason, every encounter demands that the participants assume full responsibility for themselves. If our trust is only in what we know we can expect from another, there can be no great learning. Trust, by its very nature, suggests risk.

4. *We accept our share of responsibility for every relationship.* "Well, here we are again. It's Sunday morning. I wonder what the teacher has for us today. Will I like it? Will it turn me on? Will it be the same old temperance lecture, only in different words?"

Such an attitude is an evasion. In the first place, no one can "turn you on" or "turn you off" except yourself. You are the captain of your concern, and the master of your involvement. No one is more responsible for pulling you on board than you are yourself.

If the teacher is riding "hobbies" week after week, or if the minister is preaching in such a way as to beat a dead horse week after week, then speak up. This is your *responsibility*, your ability to respond.

At the outset of all group life, it is imperative to indicate that the success and the failure of the group rests with everyone. If there is one who tends to dominate, then another member cannot escape the blame. He must accept the responsibility to encounter that individual. If someone tends to withdraw, then it must not be discussed behind that person's back. It must be dealt with. Anything less is not assuming a full responsibility for the life of the group.

Reconciliation begins by one person moving toward another in a "win/win" attitude. That step may be rebuffed: once, twice, three times, or more. But it begins with someone who will take the initiative and become involved in the hope of setting a new pace. This responsibility needs to be clear at the time of group contract.

5. *We will be open in the hope of being understood.* This does not mean open at both ends (and, therefore, not capable of holding onto anything important). It means being spontaneous, flexible, and ready to grow. It means being nondefensive, ready for encounter, and ready for change. I change every time I meet somebody. I must be ready for that kind of influence from everyone I meet. If I resist change; if I resist that kind of influence from others; if I am that defensive, then I will be locked into a very restricted world. I will also be unable to influence others. The whole action-parable process requires the participant's openness.

6. *We will seek to understand.* Many good friendships have been lost over a disagreement. When making a contract, it is especially important to indicate that a "good" relationship does not necessarily mean agreement. In the factors that really matter (trust, intimacy, and identity) we have all things in common. Beyond that, difference is not only useful but encouraged. Creativity comes in the tension created by those who are able to state different positions, but who do not find their personal security dependent upon that position. Security goes beyond ideas. Ideas, then, become grist for building emergent systems of relationship and mission.

This kind of security can be heightened by bringing persons into a healthy (mutually agreed upon) strength-block action parable.

For five or six minutes, have the group participants as individuals go off by themselves and write down all the strengths they feel they have. Move them into pairs for the next five or six minutes to test out these strengths and to extend the list. Then, for the next five or six minutes, have them write down on the opposite side of the paper those things which tend to block their use of these strengths. (We are not discussing weaknesses here.) These things may be persons, equipment, environment, feelings, intellect, health, lack of skill, or any other force that tends to hinder the use of his talents and skills. Have each one test these things out with his partner.

Then bring the pair into the group. At their invitation, have the group help the individuals further identify the strengths and blocks, expand their lists, interpret their needs, and, in general, give them feedback that will help change their behavior in the future, freeing up their strengths.

Then move back into the original pairs. Have them sit down and work out a step-by-step procedure that will enable each one to work on those blocks that keep him from using his strengths to the fullest. The partners should watch each other during the succeeding weeks to see if each is working on his new behavior and to become supportive of each other during and after the group meetings are over.

This process will help them learn to appreciate each other's differences. It will also serve to expose the resources of the group which are essential if the group is really going to use all its potential in helping each other live and learn.

7. *We will grow only as we appropriate new learnings from every experience.* No one is free until he is free to fail. To be ready to learn means to be ready to risk failure. The small group should afford everyone an opportunity to "try on new behavior" at the risk of failure. To test it out, to find out if it works, is to be like an actor in rehearsal for a stage play. He builds his confidence through practice in readiness for the grand entrance onto the real stage, the world. All persons need to feel this kind of support. Few risk "being different" without this kind of affirmation.

8. *We will find time to be alone.* In this era of "groupiness," there is a risk that the elevation of one claim may sublimate another. There must be time when a person is willing to move away *from* the group if he (she) is to be healthy. To be so dependent

upon the presence of the group for immediate satisfaction and happiness is like making a commitment to another idol. It becomes an end in itself, and, therefore, a substitute for living rather than real life. This is as bad as no group life at all. Persons who are comfortable in groups and find these groups an important part of their lives, but not *the* important part, are persons who can spend quiet moments alone without becoming desperate.

9. *We will continually test and revise our covenant, risking chaos.* A mature group is a group that can experience the loss of one or two members in the group, a change in leadership, and the addition of a new member without becoming traumatically disoriented. It can also refocus on another task without losing its cohesiveness. Every group really needs to build this kind of maturity right into the system. But the group needs to be even more radical. It may need to change completely from time to time, or even dissolve. Indeed, the group, after a period of time, may well be asked to consider its mission, to divide and grow, or to terminate. If the group has not sufficiently matured, but has only tended to solidify neurotic dependency needs, then this kind of suggestion will meet with varied, but strong, resistance.

In an age of change, all groups need to face the possibility of these severe changes. This means that ties need to be cemented between people which permit mobility. Such ties must express the essence of life and love, not utility.

Having established criteria for community change, and having concurred that we hold much in common (our need for trust, intimacy, and identity), we can now ask an imperative question that grows out of our willingness to respond to each other. What is it to which we address ourselves when our survival is no longer threatened? Can we permit each other the joy of being different?

Real meaning comes out of our differences. We are all uniquely made. For this reason we really need each other. This interdependence is another message of community.

Paul's experience with the Jerusalem church (Acts 15) is evidence enough of love's willingness to give understanding, and, with understanding, consent. Jesus' willingness to discuss the ambitions of his disciples (Mark 10:35-45), and the differences among the Pharisees and commoners (Matthew 16:1-6), are but two of his acts that indicate a willingness not only to deal with differences, but to encourage learning and, consequently, facilitation of life with them. This facing of differences is terribly threatening to those who prefer conformity. Nevertheless, difference heightens and broadens the teaching-learning encounter experience. It creates excitement and variety, creativity and movement.

God is "the same yesterday, today, and forever," but *God is also movement.* The corporate identity, once secure, is not lost in this flexibility. It is enhanced by it. Meaning itself leads to movement, for it is flexible. It changes with the times and events. The person is affected by all that takes place around him. He changes. He does not fear the change. He also experiences a pull of his destiny. "I am changing — in relationship to what?" Again, he permits the more manageable future to govern his behavior rather than the unmanageable past.

Now, let's test this out through an action parable. Have the group meet to discuss what life really means. Propose the following experience:

> You have just returned from your doctor's office. He has told you that you have six weeks to live. As you enter your home, your closest family member hands you a telegram that reads: "You have just inherited $6,000 from your aunt's estate, tax free. You will receive it by registered mail tomorrow." Consider these factors, and these factors only. You will spend one week getting your affairs in order. Now you have five weeks left. What will you do? How will you spend the money? Write your answers down.

After giving the group members ten minutes to write down some of their thoughts in key-word phrases, bring them into the group and have each one share what he has jotted down. Have the group members freely interact.

When each of the members has shared his fantasy, have the group move into threes, where they can consider what has been said in more detail. In this time of consideration raise some new questions: What does this experience tell you about your sense of values? What seems to be important to you? How is this reflected in your daily behavior? Is there a need for a change? If so, what change? What steps do you need to take to bring that change off? Will it be easy? Who can help you? Do you want to change?

This exercise can, at least, get the group thinking about the underlying values that very frequently determine the conscious personality of the individual. It has many ramifications for the group. Do not judge others. Judgment suggests the need for defense. This would force the members to move back to the more intensive regard for the survival characteristics suggested earlier. The group needs to see that individuals may be suggesting similar values through varied media.

One order of business for the group in its discovery of differences is to review the resources that are available in the group. So often, such resources are seen as "out there" beyond the group, to be called into the group at points of need. Some resources are "out there," and they need to be brought in at points of need. But there are also resources that need to be fully appraised and fairly utilized *within* the group.

There are several action-parable methods a group can use to draw out their resources. Each person in the group (class, committee, board, etc.) may be asked to write a resumé in key-word phrases indicating: (1) areas of interest, (2) areas of skill, and (3) areas of experience. Place them on newsprint and post them on the wall with everyone else's listing. Ask the group to encourage the further development of the lists (since persons tend to be somewhat timid about stating their own accomplishments). Be sure everything that is known about that person that would be helpful is listed. This is a concentration of strengths, resources, and skills. (Do not overlook those who have particular skills in home care, child rearing, etc.) Discuss how these resources can be used. Openly work through the question of assumptions regarding responsibility. Agree along the way that all decisions are subject to review, and that assignments are certainly to be clarified with care at the time that they are made, and later, as the task proceeds. If anyone, at any time, has any feelings about the interpretation of the assignment, how far another is going with the assignment, and wants clarification, it is his responsibility to raise the concern to the group. To hold back would be a violation of the group trust.

An alternate action-parable method for exploring, discovering, and learning how to appropriate differences is through the use of fantasy, crayon (paints), and art work. Ask the group to divide into subgroups and close their eyes. "As you think about yourself in the total group, what color comes to mind that reflects your feelings?" The color represents the individual's contribution to this group. "Select a crayon that most nearly approximates the color you have envisioned." Pass out a variety of crayons to insure a broad selection.

"Now, using your crayon and newsprint, without discussing anything (that is, remain nonverbal), draw a single picture that represents the total group feeling." Allow seven or eight minutes for the drawing. Then invite them to reflect upon what has been done.

Ventilate: How do you feel?

Identify: What happened?

Analyze: What was helpful? What was not helpful? What was the result? Be specific in asking questions about how the resources were used. Did everyone become involved? Realistically? Or did you simply opt for equity regardless of the task you decided upon? Is equitable use really equitable? Do you have a house with two green, one red, and one yellow side, a purple chimney, and orange grass? What does this mean? Equality? Mutuality? Sharing? Can we be equitable, mutual, sharing, and still be selective?

Generalize: What have you learned that you can use another time?

Now is that "other time." Ask the same subgroups to take six minutes to discuss (no drawing) what they will do a second time, using their own selected color. Discover what color resources they have. Are there possible combinations that can make colors they are missing? What kind of picture do they want to draw?

After six minutes, call them to silence and begin the drawing (all nonverbal). Give them eight minutes. "Now, sit back and look at your drawing. Compare it with the first." Internalize. Share with your group.

Ventilate. Identify. Analyze. Generalize.

Post the learnings on newsprint where they can be readily viewed. Then, bring the subgroups together, suggesting that they use these learnings as criteria for discovering what resources the group has in its membership. Ask them to develop a list for each person, and post those lists. Let other subgroups take the time to read the information. You may want to draw up a total group list of available resources.

This process should: (1) increase the awareness of the group members of their own internal resources based on unique skill and personal talents; (2) reveal points of weakness indicating the need for either the development of or the securing of other needed resources; and (3) increase the feeling that uniqueness is essential to both excitement and variety in group life. Difference can bring meaning and a sense of reality and utility to each person involved.

It extends the community beyond the need for mutual support. At this point, the community becomes an agent of change and reconciliation in a world of desperate need. It finds its mission. That is the beginning of response.

8. FEEDBACK:
LEVELING AND ENCOUNTER

In the spirit of what has preceded regarding trust, control, inclusion, and response, it is important to include here a discussion related to another basic element of human relations skill and theory: feedback.

Few have dealt with the interpersonal theory as carefully as Dr. Joseph Luft in the recent publication, *Of Human Interaction*.[3] I will not attempt to reiterate his theoretical base except to develop a brief adaptation of the theory for our purpose of discussing the whole area of feedback and its role in the human encounter.

For purposes of understanding, the self can be represented by a window divided into quadrants.

The *first* quadrant represents the self that has been made *public*. It is readily known to self and others. It is accessible and openly recognized as "the self." The *second* quadrant is the *hidden* self; the self that I know, and no one else generally knows. This sector remains a mystery unless I decide to let it be known. The *third* quadrant is the *blind;* or what I call, coupled with quadrant number one, the *actual* self. This is the self that comes through to another and determines the other's response and/or reaction: acceptance, rejection, or neutrality. It cannot be known without some responsive feedback from others who observe and interact with us. The *fourth* quadrant is the *unconscious*. This quadrant remains unknown to a degree to all of us. It is the heart of our motivation and drive. It is encompassed by our inner defenses. It is especially important to anyone who wishes to serve self and others consciously, for it requires the development of good intrapersonal communications between the parts of the self, not the least of which, are the motives.

In a given encounter, the self offers feelings and information

[3] Joseph Luft, *Of Human Interaction* (Palo Alto, California: National Press Books, 1969).

from quadrant *two* to others. The measure of his offering invites a reciprocal amount of feedback from others. Most people tend to be closed up. They offer little. They get back little. Quadrant *one* determines the size and shape of every other quadrant in the self.

DIAGRAM A

The Self

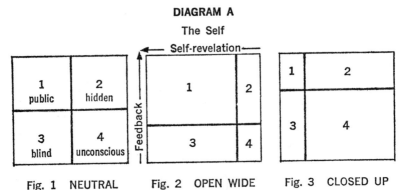

Fig. 1   NEUTRAL   Fig. 2   OPEN WIDE   Fig. 3   CLOSED UP

The more we offer, the greater the solicitation of feedback. The self discovers more and more of itself in each encounter, making the unconscious more available to the self for professional use. It becomes more and more apparent: a professional is one who can make good conscious use of himself in any given situation. Quadrant *one* is enlarged with each new invitation to encounter.

The open person is ready for learning that can and will affect his behavior. He is open to change. When the reverse is true there is little fertile ground for implanting new ideas. Such a restricted person will be very anxious. He may appear to be open (back-slapping); but all he does is send up a smoke screen to cover his real self. He may appear withdrawn, but this is in the hope of being left alone. Both the aggressor and the withdrawn (fight-flight) persons are inviting encounter by their behavior. But encounter can only come when the conditions are right.

When are conditions right for encounter?

First, there must be established a basic rapport between all of the persons involved which suggests that they have developed a secure relationship of trust. This relationship, of course, can never be guaranteed. Sometimes what appears to be a healthy mutual-adult relationship will break down when one person is unwilling to continue the adult interpersonal action.

On occasion, the teacher-learner may be responsible for a premature encounter. This is a risk. He will need to be ready to say, "O.K., I'm wrong!" He may need to ask forgiveness; pull some new learnings; sharpen his skills; and press on. But he cannot, in good conscience, ignore it. There is an ethical concern that warrants respect.

Second, an encounter should occur in circumstances most conducive to good learning. A good "bawling out" for a teenager in front of his peers, a "dressing down" of a foreman before his laborers, a "cutting up" of a minister in front of his congregation, can only result in general disaster, *regardless of the previous relationship.* An encounter in private, or a small group encounter, may permit an open flow of understanding, unimpeded by intrapersonal and interpersonal blocks, that can become learnings for everyone involved.

Third, the one who confronts must learn how to confront — by leveling, not by clobbering. This needs to be learned by church leaders: clergy and laymen alike. What we feel is in the best interest of another often comes out as a clobbering (usually read as hostility or overcriticism).

For example, one young wife, terribly threatened by an encounter, struck back at her husband with a vehemence. She told him in no uncertain terms that he was incompetent to judge her, incompetent to be a husband and father, and what is more, she should have married a man! She clobbered him! The object? To emasculate him! He held his ground. In quieter moments he responded, "I love you — in your anger and in your joy. I feel that you want very much to put me down, to emasculate me! I can't have that! Will you work with me on those feelings along with whatever other feelings you have?"

"Yes," she replied. "I felt that you were very threatening when you criticized my work and my family. I became angry with you, and wanted to hurt you. I don't know why I became so angry!"

"I became defensive, too, when you started swinging. I guess I was angry, too!"

This was not the end of this conversation. It went on. With more help, resolve came. The two persons found a mutual encounter possible by: (1) learning to level; (2) being receptive to a confrontation; and (3) responding in an encounter.

Leveling means being ready both to accept the full responsibility for what you are going to say and to give the hearer full range of freedom from which to respond. That is: "I feel," not "You should have"; "I am concerned," not "You should be concerned."

A confrontation implies that both parties turn toward each other at the invitation of the leveler. The leveling is an initiating act. It ends in a mutual encounter. They "face together" the matters at hand. There is no put down, no cutting up, no judgment.

The encounter is developed as the dialogue moves along toward some purposeful resolve. In the case of the husband and wife above, the movement was toward the resolve of angry feelings. Later, they dealt with the factors that led to these feelings in the first place. There is always satisfaction in this meeting. Many go away feeling alive and fresh after such an encounter is completed. (If you always go away exhausted and dead, something is going wrong. Are you really meeting each other, or are you trying to maintain your image so that image meets image? There is no resolve here!)

As with everything else, there are ground rules for offering feedback to someone else.

1. *Feedback is descriptive rather than evaluative.* By describing one's own reaction, the individual is freed to use the information or not to use it as he sees fit. Avoiding evaluative language reduces the need for the individual to react defensively.

2. *Feedback is specific, not general.* To be told that one is "dominating" will probably not be as useful as to be told that "just now, when we were deciding the issue, you did not listen to what others said. I felt forced to accept your arguments or face an attack from you."

3. *Feedback takes into account the needs of both the receiver and giver of feedback.* Feedback can be destructive when it serves only the giver's needs and fails to consider the needs of the person on the receiving end.

4. *Feedback is directed toward behavior about which the receiver can do something.* Frustration is only increased when a person is reminded of some shortcoming over which he has no control.

5. *Feedback is solicited, not imposed.* Feedback is more useful when the receiver himself has formulated the kind of question which those observing him can answer.

6. *Feedback is well timed.* In general, feedback is more useful at the earliest opportunity after the given behavior (depending, of

course, on the person's readiness to hear it, support available from others, etc.) is manifested.

7. *Feedback is checked to insure that the communication is clear.* One way of doing this is to have the receiver try to rephrase the feedback he has received to see if it corresponds to what the sender had in mind. When feedback is given in a personal encounter group, *both the giver and the receiver have the opportunity to check the accuracy with others in the group.* Is this one man's impression, or is it an impression that is shared by others?

Feedback is a way of giving help. It is a corrective mechanism for the individual who wants to learn how well his behavior matches his intentions. It is a means for establishing one's identity; for answering "Who am I?"

There are several ways to ask this question. Ask the group to take time, in five minutes of silence, to look at each person in the group. Then take a 3 x 5 card for each person in the group. If there are fifteen persons, each one will have fifteen cards. Put the name of each person on the top of a separate card. (Hold on to the fifteenth card for your own summary.)

Now, encourage each one to take whatever time he needs to answer the following questions, using key word phrases. If anyone refuses to do this, it should be a signal to the others to eliminate his card. No feedback should be imposed. The leader might explicitly ask: "Is there anyone who would prefer not to have feedback? If so, we will eliminate his card, and, in turn, will not solicit his feedback for others."

1. "You are most helpful to me when _____."
2. "You are not very helpful to me when _____."
3. "Right now, I feel _____ (toward you)."
4. "Your role in this group seems to be _____."
5. "I have the following concerns about you _____."

After these cards are completed, pass them to the person whose name is on the card. BE SURE EVERYONE SIGNS HIS CARD. Identification of feedback is extremely important. Let each one read his cards through to himself. Then write on the fifteenth card a summary of how others see him in light of the questions asked. Note any feelings, responses, questions for clarification, and thoughts on that card that the respondent wants to work with. Internalize.

Then share. (If someone does not want to share at this point, respect that person, but take careful note that feedback has been given and something may have blocked the follow-through.) Be sure that there is ample time for everyone to respond.

Other means for feedback are possible. To have partners or the whole group assign a color, a game, an animal, a car, a flower, a punctuation mark, or to build a house for a person is helpful. To develop a group collage for each person, using magazine cutouts (or drawings) discovered by the persons responding to the person, can give one an appropriate multiple-response.

In every feedback situation, ample time needs to be given for a full response and the resolve of feelings.

Why are we concerned about feedback in a book about experiential education?

The key to all learning is the learner. Like the sower who knowingly sows, we must turn the earth before we can hope for new life and growth. Actually, all human relations skills are TOOLS (and tools *only*) for churning the earth, planting new ideas through experience, and nurturing the growth of those new ideas. Trust, inclusion, response, and feedback are vitally important to this process. Anything less may lead to either no life or a short life. Can we pour new wine into old wineskins? Most of our teaching-learning efforts may really come to naught if the learner is unprepared.

In the parable of the sower, Jesus revealed that he was aware of the need to prepare the ground for the seed. Jesus was the master teacher-learner. His tools were the tools of love; now they are also the tools of the Christian who dwells as his embodiment in the fellowship of the church.

In the church these very skills can immeasurably facilitate the coming of God's kingdom if and when the teacher-learner has equipped himself in the skill and practice of experiential education.

PART III
The Application in a Church Setting

9. SMALL GROUP LIFE IN THE CHURCH

Experiential education is the major contemporary tool for nurturing the churchman of the Christian movement. Everything, if it is to be really learned, must be experienced. The church must facilitate the experiences which its communicants need for their spiritual growth. The church school may well be only one intermediary phase of the Christian's full development, no phase being lesser than any other. Preaching, visiting, studying, and serving are all intricately related to experiencing the gospel of Jesus Christ. The small group is one means to this experiential action. There are others. But the small group harbors important power both for evangelism and mission.

Like the family, the small encounter group has its place, serves its purpose; and either may fade out or be replaced by several other kinds of encounter groups as the consequence of the first group's success. The small group is a style of evangelism which changes lives. To the Christian, the framework of the group is God's as revealed in Jesus Christ through the church. How does the small group function within the church? What do we need to do to facilitate small group life in a local church?

There are many kinds of groups that exist within the church. Not all groupings are the same, but all groupings hold an equal importance to those persons who are involved in them. Someone may say, "But being a part of a fellowship group is certainly more challenging than being a part of a social group!" That may be true — for *that* person. But it may not be true for another who feels that just experiencing some groupness in an open-contact group is all the groupness he can handle at that moment. And it may be all he needs. No one type of group can be rated against another as "good," "better," or "best." A group finds validity in its ability to meet the needs of the persons involved.

1. *Contact Groups:* These groups vary in size and regularity

of meeting. They often meet weekly (or biweekly) giving the invited persons an opportunity to meet others, generally their peers, in an unstructured setting where little is required of them. General conversation, the sharing of an interest, or participation in a general activity where the individual can choose whether he will be in or out of the action, is the usual format. There is little or no pressure to belong or to take some responsibility for the group life.

2. *Social Groups:* These groups vary in size and regularity of meeting. They may be open or closed groups, depending on the purpose and constituency. These groups are generally self-selective, and permit a growing sense of "belongingness" on the part of the participants. Based on an interest or a common concern, individuals are encouraged to meet for fun and pleasure. Leadership comes from the group itself in order to give direction and meaning to their togetherness. These groups are generally supportive in a social way. New faces are added. Old ones are lost without much fanfare.

3. *Interest Groups:* These groups are something more than the traditional "class" groups that have met in the church. Rather there is a specific effort made in these groups to build a sense of trust and inclusiveness that will lead to a climate of openness, leading to understanding that permits serious intellectual questioning, doubting, and argument. It is usually focused on content (substantive) matters.

4. *Fellowship Groups:* These groups do not exclude the above factors of importance. Fellowship groups specifically include: (a) a sense of commitment to the group life, (b) focus on considerations to which the group gives its attention beyond "just meeting," (c) concern for each other, including a ministry to each other on critical occasions, and (d) a more deliberate sharing of intimacies and personal aspects of life. There is a "family feeling" of "we are in this together." This kind of group meets regularly (weekly is best) and tends to be very supportive. It is generally lay-dominated and lay-oriented. Books that consider biblical, historical, theological, sociological, psychological, and other current concerns are often used as a common jumping-off place for discussion, which soon becomes personal, here and now, and intimate. These groups enter a common discipline together that may include: (a) daily prayer for each other, (b) daily Scripture reading, (c) regular weekly worship, (d) disciplined study, and (e) regular service involvements.

This kind of group is the level to which the church must primarily address itself. It is both the community that develops from commitment and the mission that grows out of caring. The first group styles tend to grow toward the fellowship group. The latter group styles, listed below, tend to feed back into the fellowship group.

5. *Encounter Groups:* These groups are different from those suggested above. They play an important role in our churches. Encounter groups are called human relations groups, training groups, sensitivity groups, leader development groups, or dialogue groups. These groups meet a very special human need in our day. Whether they are single, brief, weekend encounters or weekly meetings spread over the year, they help encourage personal growth and human interaction in exciting ways. Special leadership is required. Specially prepared trainers serve as enablers to help the participants to: (a) explore the whole area of human relations, (b) explore and discover new ways to behave, (c) be aware of the group processes, (d) develop new skills in various areas of human interaction, such as conflict management, team building, curriculum development, strategic planning, creative innovation, and/or organizational development.

Ultimately, this kind of group life contributes a great deal to the development of strong, sensitive church leadership. Meetings are intensely personal. They focus on the here and now, test once-adhered-to boundaries, and permit exploration and discovery in the new, untried world of the human potential. Related to the gospel, such a group creates an atmosphere wherein a deep abiding fellowship is encouraged very similar to the development of Jesus' team of disciples. Meaning becomes the primary concern for living. Its major objective is to train leaders who can move back into the fellowship and offer both life and skill to the service of God and man.

6. *Therapy Groups:* The popular use of the word "therapy" has led many to avoid this kind of encounter. This is too bad! The word simply means "healing." It implies soundness, wholeness, and freedom. There are many in our churches who need this kind of a settling encounter. It permits persons to explore their hang-ups in a controlled environment, allowing for decision as to whether one wants really to change the old patterns of interaction or reinforce them. A therapy group leads to greater understanding of those dynamic factors that so strongly influence our behavior and

affect (or infect) our group involvements. These groups often last for two years and are considered closed groups (i.e., one attends by invitation only). There is generally a strong commitment to the group, assuring everyone of a 100 percent attendance on all occasions. Feelings are freely exposed, while a supportive group offers sensitive feedback. Trained professional leadership is required and can be secured only at a high price. (Those who are involved in this should be willing to pay those costs.)

The action parable is used to one degree or another on all six levels of group involvement, with modifications at each level. The motive and expected outcome generally define the depth of the use of the action parable. A skilled teacher will know the level of intensity each style of group meeting suggests and will modify the action accordingly. Less skillful leaders will not weigh the situation sufficiently, risking all kinds of unforeseen consequences without a means of restitution and/or reconciliation. The latter course needs to be discouraged.

The fellowship group is the core of the church community. It is this community that needs to reflect the modeled commitment, commission, and community life suggested by the early church initiated by Jesus and his disciples. Groups that precede this level tend to feed into the fellowship on a continuum as those persons find significant involvement and growth along the way. Those groups which are listed below the fellowship level intensify, strengthen, and direct the fellowship groups. It is at the fellowship level that we find the embodiment of the church.

> By this we may be sure that we are in him: he who says he abides in him ought to walk in the same way in which we walked. . . . He who says he is in the light and hates his brother is in the darkness still. He who loves his brother abides in the light . . . (1 John 2:5-10).

The fellowship *is* the embodiment of the relational theology. To feel that one has lived without ever finding this love relationship is to live only with the veil of a grand illusion. There has been no recent student of psychology or sociology who has dared imply that a man can be a person alone. Only another human can call a being into being. If one cannot believe in his fellowman, whom he can see, how, then, can he ever believe in a God whom he cannot see? And if he says he loves God and hates his brother, he is a liar (see 1 John 2).

The end of our own self-knowledge is to be more consciously aware of how we use ourselves in all our intimate "belonging" relationships. The learning tasks themselves are projected in behavioral terms that require relationships for learning. Learning *is* relational: listen, respond, explore, discover, appropriate, and assume responsibility. These are action thrusts — action that catches up the person in relationships.

The model for this small group action-centered learning comes to us out of the Acts of the Apostles. The disciples met, planned, and projected their destiny. They acted, moved, and converted. They nurtured, conserved, and committed. These developments excited every man who came within its purview. Modern planning and designing is called ACTION-RESEARCH. Everything that happens becomes grist for learning. The "stuff" of the personal, social, political, economic, educational, vocational, recreational, and historical worlds merges in one gigantic effort. Each person reaches out to every other person in a relationship of trust, hoping to be heard, hoping to discover, hoping to grow. Everyone becomes, then, a teacher, just as everyone has become a learner. And all of this happens best in a community, a fellowship of caring. Everyone in this kind of group life reflects those characteristics which we once felt only the designated leader should reflect:

1. a clear vision of the results intended;
2. a fertile imagination;
3. a personal security and a willingness to trust;
4. a confidence in the gospel he teaches;
5. an awareness of the relationship between what he teaches and what the real life issues are; and more important
6. a saturation with the mind of Jesus Christ.

The intensity of the small fellowship group encourages the emergence of these qualities.

These small groups will be committed to a common faith, a common framework, and a common discipline for interaction. They may also be known as covenant groups. The common faith will find simplification in the biblical affirmation that "Jesus Christ *is* Lord." The common framework will begin with the biblical message, with the Four Gospels as the central concern. It will include the life and works of men who have remained faithful to that biblical message through the 2000 years or more. A common discipline will be developed more as a means to an end than as an end in itself.

"Discipline" appears to be a hard word. But it carries with it the promised abundant life. Life must be disciplined, if it is to move at profound depths. Life must have some intensity if it is to be creative. How can a group covenant to work together in the here and now and with creative intensity? For the Christian in fellowship, there are several possibilities:

1. *A common prayer life* — to learn to pray for each other in specific terms, with brevity, but with commitment.
2. *A common study of the Scripture* — to learn and study the Scriptures (committed to an understanding borne in the question: how would my life be different if I really lived that Scripture?).
3. *A common life* — how shall we relate to one another? Can we covenant together to share on a level of mutual trust, openness, and responsibility to the end that we may come to understand one another? Can we interact in the here and now? Will we pledge responsible participation in the group life?
4. *A common development* — can we discover the resources existent within the group, develop them further, and make room for individuals to use and reinforce those learning skills in group action elsewhere?
5. *A common concern* — to what end do we come together? Can we relate what we do in life in the world?

How can we start small groups in the church? Right away, we need to put aside the old "bigger 'n' better" adage. A group may begin with from eight to twelve persons (and no more). It is better to begin to develop a group with three well-intentioned persons who can heighten the encounter because of who they are, than to begin nominally with dozens who come with reservations. Intimacy always begins small, usually with one other person.

We must recognize that it takes time to move into a deeper level of human relationships. Jesus knew this ever so well. He spent three years working intensely with a small group of twelve men. A minimum of time required to begin a ministry of small group life is eighteen months to two years. The group should meet weekly for two or more hours.

The leadership will be shared, but it will be initiated by one or two caring facilitators. The most open person, and his openness may be limited, will set the norms for the group interaction. There may be resistance at first. Respect it. This resistance will tend to neutralize whatever efforts are made to move toward a greater trust and openness. But patience and persistence will endure.

Church leaders who are interested in the development of groups may want to call in a consultant (or a small group of consulting lay leaders who have known success in establishing small group encounters). A living witness always helps motivate the skeptic who wants to be shown. Usually, the overflow of lives touched by this process is enough, at least, to encourage another to hear what is being said.

The important factors to remember about small group learning are:

1. There is validity in all human community life.
2. Community has the potential of changing life.
3. Community can extend its limits as far as its vision.
4. There is a similarity between what persons do in groups and what they do in the world.

Knowing these things, the church has within its grasp the potential for affecting lives permanently; for setting the world on its end for Christ's purposes. The small group movement is that kind of tool.

10. TEAM BUILDING

"It's a whole new ball game," Jim announced to his wife, Betty, when he arrived home from the church school leaders' retreat. "I've been teaching church school for seven years, and I never knew that it could be fun; that it could bring a new point of view to my faith; or that it could help me find support for my personal, professional, and church life. I'm really excited about what happened today."

I wonder if this will last, Betty was asking herself. I've seen Jim turned on before. Not quite as much — but some! There was a period just following his initial commitment to teach. He was all fired up with great plans. That waned in three months. The training program didn't work out. The young people had so many Sunday conflicts. They were so busy that they couldn't even find time for a social evening. When Jim got discouraged, the pastor handed him some books with a slap on the back, saying, "Buck up, Jim! Buck up!" He's worked on it. His third year was pretty good. He had a responsive class. But each year he tries to give it up, only to find that no one will pick it up. He feels stuck with it. Maybe this is a new turn. Maybe! But I have my doubts.

"We had some help today," Jim went on. "The pastor asked a consultant to visit us from the regional office. His aim was to build a leader team for our church education program. Here, Betty, these were our goals for today. We developed them with the leader."

Betty looked at Jim's notes, clearly written on a well-doodled scratch pad:

- to increase our awareness of our role as designated leaders using an experiential education curriculum
- to build a leader team for mutual support and continued development
- to develop skills in problem-solving and decision-making

that will facilitate the experiential process of learning in the classroom

Jim went on into the night explaining to Betty the activities of the day; a long Saturday that really began Friday evening at the church when the teachers met with the consultant to get a glimpse of what could be, what the participants really wanted as their goals for the all-day encounter, and to begin the first stages of process awareness: becoming more aware of oneself and each other. Everyone arrived on time (8:30 A.M.), and everyone stayed through to the end (9:30 P.M.). Everyone appeared to be as involved as Jim. It was evident that this was just a beginning.

There are at least three ways to teach in the church school. The teacher can be totally concerned about the substantive matters of the lesson and insist that his teaching of content material is the most important thing. His task is to disseminate information, to get the facts across to the student as easily as possible and with reasonable accuracy. On the other hand, the teacher can be totally concerned about process matters and can spend a great deal of time and energy working out lesson plans filled with gimmicks that will hold the student's interest, activities that will keep a learner busy, and a variety of things that will keep the class participants entertained. The tendency is to allow one force or the other to take over. The art of working on both tracks is very difficult and comes only to the well-disciplined teacher-learner. This teacher-learner operates with dual controls: substantive and procedural. He is concerned about both the message and the media. He is convinced that they are so interwoven as to greatly influence each other in the end product. This means that he cannot teach alone. He must work (a) with many teacher resources and (b) with the learners as fellow teachers.

"There's this exercise he called an action parable," Jim recounted, "that was kind of fun, and yet made its point. Ten of us stood up in two rows, facing each other. The first row had the line, 'Where have you been?' The second row had the line, 'I came as quickly as I could.' We had to put different inflections in our question or response. Each said it, as if

1. a parent speaking to a naughty child,
2. a lover speaking to his beloved,
3. a patient speaking to the doctor,

    4. a wife speaking to her husband,

    5. an employer speaking to a late employee.

After the sensible responses, he mixed them up. What we have been doing all these years really became apparent in the humor of it all."

"We went on to discuss the task (substantive), and what he called the maintenance (process) functions of group life. I saw my class for the first time as a team, a group. In fact, we talked about three kinds of teams or groups today: the church as a whole, the church school leader team, and our classes. That's been my trouble. I've never seen any of these groups, let alone my class, as a team. They have just been a bunch of young people."

Team building is concerned about all levels of group interaction. We seldom recognize large groups as teams. We seldom see any group, other than an athletic group, as a team. We usually think about a team as being small, three or four, ten or twelve, persons involved in a sports event, or a contest. Not much more. And yet, in the best sense of the word, every citizen of the United States is a part of a team; a big team. We win and we lose, together. The principles of teammanship are not related to the team's size.

1. Every team member is essential to the life of the team. Teamwork is a shared quest.

2. Every team member plays a role in affecting the team task positively or negatively.

3. Leadership is emergent (grows out of the team life).

4. The higher the investment in the team life and work, the greater the risks, the greater the satisfactions in success, and the greater the disappointments in failure.

5. The team will move only as quickly as its slowest member.

6. Growth is often interrupted temporarily by personal doubt, suspicion, and distemper. But such interruptions *can be* launching pads for new surges in development.

7. A team develops, consciously or unconsciously, its own norms for operating.

8. A team must continually attend to both the task and maintenance functions or risk losing its life.

For our purposes, we are talking about the small team reflected in the church's small group movement: a small group of church leaders, a small class (8-15 persons), or even a class of sixty persons who will, from time to time, be encouraged to form small encounter groups (6-8 persons) within the larger group in order to do the more intensive work. Jesus saw *the team* as twelve men, with several others, men and women, interacting now and then with them. He saw the team as a vital instrument in building the kingdom enterprise.

Let us consider each principle at greater length:

1. *Every team member is essential to the life of the team. Teamwork is a shared quest.*

"I am a person essential to the ongoing life of this team. I will be missed if I am not present. I am heard when I am present. I belong!"

In our world, this feeling often escapes us. Few feel either this kind of investment or contentment. The small group, when it feels that it is a team, does experience this belonging. It is important for the individual member who wants to feel both safe and needed.

This means that the team has two very important responsibilities related to its membership. First, it must function as an instrument of awareness. The feedback system must work continually to keep each member consciously aware of himself and his role in the interaction of the group. This maintenance function will be more fully considered in a later principle. The second responsibility is for the further development of member skills essential for the task defined by the group as theirs.

The win/win expectation is essential for good teamwork. Any marital or family team, any athletic team, any task force team that is divided against itself cannot really win. They may achieve some success. They may even win some medals; but there is no permanent joy in them.

An athlete boasted of his professional prowess in words that reflected arrogance and condescension, directed not only toward the opponents, but also toward his fellow teammates. It was a painful evening when his team forfeited the game because the teammates, tired of his arrogance, called in sick. He could not win alone. In fact, he couldn't even play.

Most good hockey teams can do little more than play a defensive game with one or two other teammates in the penalty box. Every man on the ice counts if the game is to be exciting.

How can we meet these conditions for teamwork in the church? How can we face the frightening forces of our age — change, violence, speed, and depersonalization — without losing our potential force? Can we really effect a meaningful transition in this urbanized whirlpool of poverty and wealth, educated and uneducated, militance and backlash? How?

If it took Jesus *and* the disciples to begin the kingdom process reflected in the Gospels and the early church, if he never intended the church mission to be a "one man show," then, we need to learn how to work more as a team. For three, close, intimate years, Jesus demonstrated, taught, and questioned the disciple-team. But it has never been a simple matter, persuading men and women of the church to work as a team.

Thus man is really a social animal. He requires community. Needless to say, the man who desires maturity will choose carefully those upon whom he will depend: in marriage, in education, in religious commitment, in social ties, in political expression and in economic enterprises. Each dependency will affect him for years to come.

Our age demands this kind of interdependent maturity: a community where the concern for the whole is primary. This is one reason why businessmen, management, educators, government leaders, and social leaders are spending thousands of dollars to train people in the art of teammanship. The church, as a change agent in the world, will need to know how to put into reality the principle of discipleship through a team effort too.

Group life requires something more than "good leadership." Groups do not become a cohesive force without some purpose or focus for being. Groups meet for a variety of reasons: to persuade, to protect, to educate, to treat, to explore, to advise, to administer, to coordinate, to integrate. The level of thrust toward a group goal will determine the intensity of cohesion. An intensely personal and common purpose, meaningfully projected, serves any group or team well.

When a group is really a team, the persons who make up that group are always assured of their personhood. They do not have to risk the invalidation of their own identity for the sake of the group. Instead, the reverse is true. The group validates them as persons. Their uniqueness, their differences, are important resources. This, then, creates an even stronger feeling of cohesiveness, the feeling of mutuality.

Again, watch your favorite team. There may be one man designated as captain (or quarterback). There even may be a "star" player who apparently stands out among all the others. But rest assured, the whole team is important to the play. Every position is essential and every player is aware of his importance to the whole. There is a sense of being mutually involved in the action. There is no minority, no majority rule. Each consents to give everything he's got to the team. And the team finds itself strongly dependent upon that consensus.

Interdependence does not suggest indulgence or tyranny. It suggests a feeling that is so often important to any wedded relationship: "We're in this together . . . all the way."

Let's test out the ability of the team to work as a team. The following action parable describes the essential dimensions of cooperation[4] to team life.

The objectives are:

— To analyze some aspects of the problem of cooperation in solving a group problem.
— To sensitize the members to some of their own behaviors which contribute toward or hinder solving group problems.

The materials needed are: a chalkboard, chalk, eraser, or newsprint and a magic marker, one set of instructions for each five persons participating and one for the leader, one set of prepared squares for each five persons participating. (See the directions for making the sets of squares, p. 135.)

Begin the session by asking for the meaning of the word "cooperation" and for illustrations of situations which call for a cooperative effort. Insofar as possible, practical and local situations calling for a cooperative effort should be stressed — for instance, a project such as renovating a church parlor, or establishing a new mission in the inner city.

After the initial explanation of the meaning of the word "cooperation," develop from the group some of the required behaviors on the part of individuals if a cooperative effort is to be successful. The following ideas need to be brought out in the discussion:

1. There is a need for each individual to understand the total problem which must be solved.

[4] Reprinted by special permission from *Handbook of Staff Development and Human Relations Training: Materials Developed for Use in Africa* (revised and expanded edition), by Donald Nylen, J. Robert Mitchell, and Anthony Stout (1967), pp. 143-146.

2. There is a need for each individual to see how he can contribute toward solving the total problem.
3. There is a need for each individual to be aware of the potential contributions of other individuals in solving the problem.
4. There is a need to see the other individual's and one's own problems in order that all may be helped to make a maximum contribution.

As a leader, one may need to develop illustrations in concrete form if there is difficulty in pulling these ideas out of the group.

When the above points have been listed, indicate that the plan is to conduct an experiment to test these ideas. Divide the total group into subgroups of five persons each. Suggest that one member distribute an envelope to each of the five persons in a subgroup. Indicate that the packets are to be left unopened until the signal to begin working is given.

Call for questions of clarification. Point out that each group has a copy of the instructions in case anyone wishes to refer to them. Refer to the points which have been listed.

Give the signal to begin. By observing the groups at work, you may also collect data which will be useful for raising questions during the discussion to follow.

(Note: It is necessary to monitor the groups to reinforce the rules which have been laid down in the instructions.)

When several groups have solved the problem (or the maximum allowable time has elapsed), call time and engage the group in a discussion of the experience. The leader may allow the groups to discuss the experience among themselves before calling for general discussion.

Ventilate. Identify. Analyze. Generalize.

This action parable involves so much interest and feeling that the group discussion usually carries itself. As the leader, you may need to guide the focus of comments.

The discussion should go beyond the relating of experiences and general observations. Some important questions are: How did members feel when someone holding a key piece did not see the solution? How did members feel when someone had completed his square incorrectly and then sat back with a self-satisfied smile on his face? What feelings did they think he had? How did members feel about the person who could not see the solution as quickly as the others?

When the discussion is underway, raise questions which stimulate the participants to relate their feelings and observations to their back-home experiences.

In summarizing, the leader briefly stresses the relationship of the experiences with squares and the discussion of the points which were previously developed and listed.

Instructions to the Group: In this package are five envelopes, each of which contains pieces of cardboard for forming squares. When the leader gives the signal to begin, the task of your group is to form five squares of equal size. The task will not be completed until each individual has before him a perfect square of the same size as that held by others.

Specific limitations are imposed upon your group during this exercise:

1. No member may speak.
2. No member may ask another member for a card or in any way signal another person to give him a card.
3. Members may, however, give cards to other members.

Directions for Making a Set of Squares: One set should be pro-

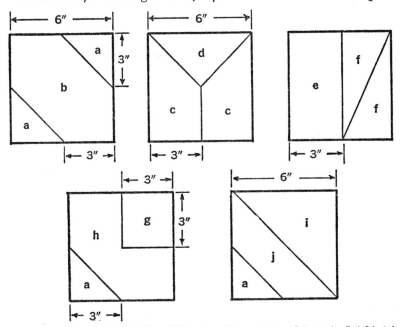

vided for each group of five persons. A set consists of five envelopes containing pieces of cardboard which have been cut into different patterns and, when properly arranged, will form five squares of equal size. To prepare a set, cut five cardboard squares of equal size, 6 x 6 inches. Place the squares in a row and mark them as below, penciling the letters *a, b, c,* and so forth, on lightly so they can later be erased.

Mark each of five envelopes A, B, C, D, and E. Distribute the cardboard pieces in the five envelopes as follows:

Envelope A has pieces *i, h, e*

Envelope B has pieces *a, a, a, c*

Envelope C has pieces *a, j*

Envelope D has pieces *d, f*

Envelope E has pieces *g, b, f, c*

Erase the penciled letter from each piece and write, instead, the appropriate envelope letter, as Envelope A, Envelope B, and so on. This will make it easy to return the pieces to the proper envelope for subsequent use.

2. Every team member plays a role in affecting the team task: positively or negatively.

Not every team member can help the team win. Some members of a team are undisciplined, untrained, and sometimes just awkward. How do we cope with that? If every team member needs to feel needed and a part of the action, how do we arrange for these more inept members? Give them busy work? Create new needs for them?

Whatever is done, it must be "for real." To give members busy work or to create needs is soon to communicate to them the rejection that is intended. I believe that any awkward situation is the business of the whole team, including the person directly concerned. He may be offended at the inference, wanting to be protected from the hard reality of the world, but no one gains or learns from being treated as someone less than a whole adult person. This open discussion can lead to a genuine resolve because everyone involved in the encounter has something at stake. Persons who tend to block team development are generally reacting to the immediate situation because of the intense similarities noted in events in their past. Not every team member can develop every kind of skill. Once in a while, an unusual team member arrives who appears to be able in most areas. But he, too, has limits. We must be taught to live with our limits. Such learning intensifies the possibilities for development in other, more accessible areas.

In recent months, an administrator shared in a team-building experience with some of his fellow educator-administrators. For ten years, he had been giving advice and spouting off great swirls of philosophical verbiage in front of his colleagues. In the encounter, he discovered, much to his humiliation, that his colleagues had heard him all these years, with tongue in cheek. They had dismissed his advice and turned off his verbiage with "Oh, that's Charlie!" and a chuckle. This new awareness resulted in a tremendous eruption of bitterness which was later resolved:

> You mean to tell me that we have been friends for ten years and you have been aware of my foolishness for that long? You never told me! You have laughed at me from the safety of your hidden reflections; and that you did this together, no less! For ten years! I've been a fool for ten years, and not one of you cared enough for me to tell me! I am deeply wounded. I'm bitter!

Every team member has a right to hear from the others on the team how he is doing as far as they are concerned. This is an important function of the team interaction.

3. Leadership is emergent.

Every team has a "captain" of sorts, someone who calls the team together, who has the respect and sanction of the other team members, and who serves in behalf of the team in outside negotiations. He may not even be the elected chairman, captain, or president, but he is present if the team is really a team. When he speaks, he is heard. When another speaks, he listens. When there is a decision to be made, his will usually expresses the thinking of others.

The best leaders in team play are aware of their limited influence. They learn to serve as facilitators, encouraging others to give leadership in moments that require what they have to give, regardless of how large or small. And they do this without feeling the need to control or "footnote" the contribution of others. This kind of team leadership is not easily developed.

Every new group spends considerable time working out team leadership roles. The struggle for leadership is initially a struggle for control. The initial struggle is healthy. To move into a team where only one person is unqualifiably the leader in everything is to create a one-eyed monster with a brief, voluntary allegiance. The team either gives up its voluntarism in the wake of the leader's ego-tyranny, or it falls apart in discontent.

A leader needs to know that he can depend upon the others of his team to assert themselves: (1) when they feel that their role has been presumptuously called into question, (2) when the life of the team has been threatened, and (3) when the sanctioned leader-facilitator needs to be strengthened in moments of his own doubt. This applies regularly to the teacher-learner. He needs to respect the teacher-learner role of every member in the group. He needs to be helped when what he is doing is a distortion of the group contract. He needs to be helped when his own limits have been reached.

One of the most devastating circumstances occurs when the teacher pontificates nobly, and the learner assumes that he is present to "sponge up" learning from the wiser one. Neither really learns. There may be an exchange of information, but this is not learning in the experiential sense at all. This kind of leadership needs to be challenged.

One of the most potent of all the leadership-control action parables is known as the "Stick Wield." It can (though not always) bring to the surface a person's strongest feelings about control. It requires spontaneity, innovation, and physical interaction. It can be used to work through many different kinds of control issues in group life. There must be both an agreement to enter into this encounter and ample pre-meeting time to build some legitimate channels of communication.

Take a stick (preferably made of strong material, rounded, about four feet long) and place it on the floor between four or five persons. Have the remainder of the group observe carefully what takes place. Everyone should participate in the action before discussing the action parable. Your instructions will be: "This action parable is nonverbal. You, who stand together in the center, are a group. The pole represents an issue (or a tool). Remember, this is nonverbal."

Give no further instructions. Stand back and observe. After everyone has had a chance to enter the action, take a few moments to internalize the feelings and events. Then discuss it.

Ventilate. Identify. Analyze. Generalize.

Be sure to raise such questions (during the analysis) as:
Who took the initiative in the actions?

Who worked together with whom? Against whom?

Was there any resolve of leadership?

Did various people get to do their "thing" with total group cooperation? If not, why not?

4. The higher the investment in the team life and work, the greater the risks, the greater the satisfactions in success, the greater the disappointments in failure.

A team member is one who has cast his lot with the upswing and downfall of a group. He is, of necessity, tied in with what happens to his fellow teammates. This essentially means that his life is very much dependent upon factors beyond his control: sickness, injury, disharmony, conflict, and the like. This is less true of the loner. His rising and falling is pretty much geared to his own skill and stamina. (This has its disadvantages as well as its advantages.) The team member lives by faith whether he wants to or not. He may successfully feign control for a time. But even the most astute tyrant loses hold of some things eventually.

5. The team will move only as quickly as its slowest member.

As the Cooperative Square action parable demonstrated, a team cannot move any faster than its members allow. Some would move swiftly, deliberately. Others move more slowly, less deliberately. The feelings that these differences in pace engender are sometimes overwhelming. In fact, many teams cease to exist when the tension becomes too great.

The team needs effective tools that will facilitate growth and movement while respecting the level of development achieved by the individual team member. An adequate feedback helps in this process.

6. Growth is often interrupted temporarily by personal doubt, suspicion, and distemper. But such interruptions can be launching pads for new surges of development.

Every group (of two or more persons) is plagued with stalemates and conflict. Many of us are plagued with these factors within ourselves, let alone within a team relationship. There are two basic suggestions related to this concern. First, these conflicts should be expected. They are the source of all new creative thrusts. Second, channels for resolve should be deliberately constructed before the conflict arises. (See chapter 11: Conflict Utilization)

7. A team develops, consciously or unconsciously, its own norms for operating.

These norms will help to answer questions like these:

How will we work together?

Where do I fit?

What will be the written norms of this group?

More important, what will be the unwritten norms of this group?

Can I buy in? Can I influence their development?

If the members of a group are going to live by rules, written and/or unwritten, they need to have a voice in their development. And if the roles are ever to be changed, then the group members need to have the right to help bring about that change, too.

8. A team must continually attend to both the task and the maintenance functions or risk losing its life.

The *task* is the "job" for which the team meets. It can generally be discovered in the objectives that are stated by the team members. The *maintenance* concerns relate to personal needs: will this group, its goals, and methods help each member to achieve a sense of worth and satisfaction? If so, then each member may find a place in the group. If not, they may need to look elsewhere.

This concern suggests that every team, like every group in general, needs to take the time to examine its behavior. Such self-examination should lead to new learning through a new awareness and a willingness to change the less favorable behavior. The forms on pages 141 and 142 have been used by churchmen to sample team concern and development.

No one on a team can be content "to be." Each team member must sense a need for more competence: to develop even more as a person, as a team member, and as a participant in the team enterprise. We live in a day which demands continual development. Our level of competence can never remain static. We must grow if we are to accept the challenge to make things happen consistently.

In our new life style, team members are being required to assume both personal and corporate responsibility for the growth and

WORKSHEET #1: MAINTENANCE FUNCTIONS

Member behavior that helps to build and maintain the group as a working unit	Specific examples of such behavior

1. ENCOURAGING: being friendly, warm and responsive to others; accepting others and their contributions; giving others an opportunity to speak.

2. EXPRESSING GROUP FEELINGS: sensing feeling, mood, relationship within the group; sharing one's own feelings with others as to what is happening.

3. HARMONIZING: attempting to reconcile disagreements; reducing tension through "pouring oil on troubled waters"; helping people to explore their differences.

4. COMPROMISING: when own ideas or status are involved in a conflict, offering to compromise one's own position; admitting error, disciplining oneself to maintain group cohesion.

5. GATE-KEEPING: attempting to keep communication channels open; facilitating the participation of others.

6. SETTING STANDARDS: summarizing and expressing standards by which group is to work and/or testing group behavior against such standards.

7. CHRISTIAN CONCERN: raising questions related to the purpose and framework of the Christian faith related to the group's life.

WORKSHEET #2: TASK FUNCTIONS

Member behavior that helps in doing the job in a group	Specific examples of such behavior
1. INITIATING: proposing tasks or goals; defining a problem; suggesting a procedure.	
2. INFORMING: requesting and offering facts; seeking and/or giving opinions providing information pertinent to task.	
3. CLARIFYING: interpreting ideas or suggestions; defining terms; suggesting alternatives; clearing up confusion.	
4. SUMMARIZING: pulling together related ideas; restating suggestions; offering a decision or conclusion for group to consider.	
5. CONSENSUS TRAINING: sending up "trial balloons" to see if group is nearing a conclusion; checking with others to see how much agreement has been reached.	
6. FOCUSING: helping to relate the immediate to the ongoing, overall goal of the Christian faith: "the new person in Jesus Christ."	

development of individuals and the team. To understand human development and personal growth, to gain more self-awareness in a time of change, to study organizational development and group process, to learn the strategic planning process and problem diagnosis, to understand new leader roles and administrative processes, and to develop research procedures are some of the helpful roads to greater competence. This is more than developing a competence for the enlargement of a function of the church. It is to improve those human capabilities that are so essential to every person in his everyday living and learning.

Why a team?

The forces of change are too overwhelming for one man to assume the responsible role of the "change agent" today. More often than not (though there are times when one man does make an impact) a team of dedicated persons is needed to make an impact on society, even if one man does assume the leader role. The thrust is contingent on cooperative action. Without this, little can be accomplished.

In the church, this teammanship must be reflected in several ways: (a) the professional ministry (when several churches need to have ministers work together in developing a common community work); (b) clergy-laity relations (where the task is too overwhelming for one or the other); (c) lay relations; and (d) connectional cooperativeness (for some reason, groups within the same church, or churches within the same denomination, or denominations within the same kingdom mission, have not yet learned to work together as a part of the team across the boundaries of parochial interest).

Ask your task group to work at building a team. Set aside at least three uninterrupted hours where all those who want to be a part of the team can meet together to consider their own team life. Follow the outline given below (or change it to meet your own needs and abilities):[5]

15 minutes: *Overview:* What are we here to do? Explain the need to have purpose, mutuality, and competence, if you are to be a team.

10 minutes: *Readiness Time:* Stand in a circle, and "toss in" an imaginary ball (see chapter 5 for all details).

10 minutes: *Pair off* and discuss: "Teams I have belonged to before." How did I work with these teams? How do you see yourself working on this team?

10 minutes: *Have a piece of paper and pencil ready* and, after the 10-minute discussion, put down (a) a punctuation mark that reflects how you feel about the person you have been sharing with, and (b) the color that you see him reflecting.

10 minutes: *Share the punctuation mark and color* with the group, giving whatever explanations you want. Interpretation of symbols (like color and punctuation) should be done only by the person using them. The interpretations should be brief and simple to be effective.

15 minutes: *Stand in a circle.* "This circle is the outer rim of a cartwheel. You are standing at the end of a spoke on that wheel. Move in and out on that spoke to show where you are in relation

[5] See also Nancy Geyer and Shirley Noll, *Team Building in Church Groups* (Valley Forge: Judson Press, 1970).

to the others in the group (see chapter 6 for details). After you find the place that seems best, look around. Get the picture. Let's sit down and talk about it."

15 minutes: *Group movement.* "Stand again in a circle. Put your shoulders together, close your eyes. Nonverbal. You are a wave beating on the beach." (Do this for six minutes.) "Now discuss it. Who took the initiative? Who tried to bring the group together, if anyone did? How did it feel to be bumped? What happened? Did the group become one wave? Was it gentle? Did it take long? How do you now feel about the group?" What does this say about teammanship?

10 minutes: *Lecturette:* What is a team member? Why do groups come together? Discuss briefly three essentials: (a) the individual's need to be a person, (b) the group and its process, (c) the art of sharing leadership.

50 minutes: *Cooperative Square Action Parable* in team cooperation
or
Tinker Toy Communication Action Parable. Ask the team to build something for five or six minutes using Tinker Toys. Do not discuss it or talk. What happened? Who directed it? Pull learnings. Now, for five minutes discuss a project you can complete together. Build it for the next six minutes without talking. What happened this time?
or
Draw a community picture (crayons and large sheet of drawing paper). We are going to draw a team mural. Do not talk, or discuss it. Draw for five minutes. What happened? Plan another mural for the next five minutes. Now, remain silent and draw it together. What happened this time?

How did we work together in our planning, making decisions, and executing our plans? Were we flexible? What feelings do we have right now about this team? Can I trust this team to make decisions for me? Why? Why not?

In closing this team-building experience, ask the team to work out an appropriate experience that would reflect what has happened that would be truly a celebration of how they feel "right now" about the life of the team and the mission to which they are committed in the future. Give them time to plan and an opportunity to execute their plan before another team's if it is present.

The whole team should discuss the whole experience. They will want to deal with questions like these: What have we learned about being a team? What feelings did you have as we moved from one experience to the other? What new learning will we apply in our next team encounter? How do you feel about the team now?

11. CONFLICT UTILIZATION

"Can I have three volunteers from the group? Any three! Stand up quickly! *(Pause.)* Any three!" Three members stand, one instantly, another rather questioningly, and the third after some coaxing. The other group members remain expectantly in their seats.

"O.K. Thank you! The exercise is all over," the leader continues. "Now, sit down again. I want everyone now to think through, as specifically as possible, what you went through in making your decision to volunteer or not to volunteer." There's a little group banter. Then it's quiet. "Picture in your mind what you were going through to arrive at your decision. Get the picture firmly in your mind. Internalize. Share it, if you can, verbally or non-verbally."

Pause.

Mary (who had not volunteered) spoke to Tom (who had volunteered). "You did it for me!" Tom questioned her, "Why me?"

"Because I consider you a leader in this group, and I didn't want to do it myself. I knew you would." (Pause.) John quickly added: "I wasn't fantasizing what others should do like that. I was having my own tug-of-war, right inside me. There were two sides of me, two characters, each arguing against the other. 'Go ahead, get up there. You know you always learn more when you are involved. Risk it.' The other side was saying, 'Fool! He'll put you on the spot, and you know you decided to wait it out this time.'"

"That seems right for me, too," Vicki added. "I didn't want to get pulled into something I didn't know about. If you had told us what you wanted us to volunteer for," she addressed the trainer, "I might have volunteered then. But you just asked for three volunteers."

"Well, I was going to volunteer. I even said I would. But I didn't get up. I guess I really didn't mean it. I just verbalized it."

"That's the way you always are, Bart," Tom came back. "You talk up a storm but you don't really volunteer."

"Yeah," was Bart's knowing response. He pondered Tom's statement.

"Well, I had decided before the group met that I would try anything that was going. That's why I stood up. What did I have to lose?" crowed Hank.

The group discussion continued for some minutes as the members began to sense some inner conflict and concern about their willingness or unwillingness to get involved in the unknown. They talked some about their trust level but spent most of their time considering the elements of conflict and why they tended more to "play things safe" than run the risk of encounter.

The excuses varied:

— "I avoid all conflict. It frightens me."
— "I try to be nice. I like things smooth. I say what people want to hear. Then I don't have to take any flak!"
— "I don't really care what people think. I just do what I please, and say what I please."
— "I wish people wouldn't start things like that. It makes me uncomfortable. I look around for allies. If there are enough around, I might try getting involved. But if I'm not sure, I stay out of it."
— "What conflict?"

These are all ways of coping. We learn to cope one way or another from the very first minutes of our lives. We continually test out behavior in the hope of discovering which way brings us the most pleasure and which results in the most pain. With a few exceptions (generally noted as sadistic or masochistic behavior), comfort is preferred to discomfort. Conflict and tension are avoided. "I want to find acceptance, avoid hurt, pain, rejection, encounter, disagreement. . . ."

Recently, an educator told the story of his early life in the California forests where he worked as a ranger. On one occasion after a severe fire that damaged acres of prime forest land, he hiked back into the area with a team to survey the damage and discuss alternatives to what they expected would be severe erosion. To their surprise, they found the ground covered with small green shoots that were beginning to spread over the burned out area. Now and then, they found small black seeds that could not be opened by hand. It took a blow torch to break them open. They were nema-pharia seeds, seeds that would not grow except under severe conditions, when the heat was extreme. They generally broke open during severe fires, planted themselves in the ashes, and proceeded to grow new ground cover. They were nature's answer to threatening erosion.

Strange, but true! And there are resources available to all of us in the midst of the tensions that heighten life. But they go undiscovered until an extreme condition occurs. When we consider the miraculous advances which are made during wartime, the advances during a space race, and new building developments in the midst of an urban crisis, we realize that often our most creative forces break out under pressure.

Conflict is an ingredient of growth. Yet most of us avoid it, deferring to safety. It seems to be better to "play it cool," to keep things "under control," than to be labeled a "troublemaker." Conflict is labeled "bad."

Ask your group to pull into the circle facing each other. Then consider the following facts (and accept them as facts, simulating these conditions):

> We have just been told that we must evacuate our town. There are 1,700 of us; men, women, and children. The town will be destroyed in a matter of minutes by a nearby volcanic eruption. There is a train at the station that can still get out of town through a nearby tunnel. All the other roads and byways are closed off by debris and lava. The train can hold, at most, only five hundred persons. How will you decide who goes and who does not? Who makes the decision? You have only fifteen minutes to get the plan into action. After that, it will be too late.

What conditions have been set up? What feelings can you sense as you simulate the tension of a 15-minute decision that will affect 1,700 people's lives? How must the people have felt on that terrible night when the *Titanic* went down in the waters of the Atlantic? How do we cope with severe conflict faced in moments of critical decision.

Again, there are three major ways of coping:

1. *Paralysis:* "Not having resolved the feelings and fears of the past, when something occurs, I freeze. I am rendered helpless."

2. *Computerized:* "When something occurs, I run through the experiences of the past looking for a relevant hook. And if I find something that looks like this situation, I try it. Otherwise, I'm lost."

3. *Actualized:* "In any event, large or small, I use whatever wit I have at that moment, and work to resolve the condition by immediate action regardless of the circumstances. I do my best."

Many persons respond to life in a "someday I'm going to" spirit. They talk about all those intended events and happenings but never move decisively to an action. They fear the consequences. Therefore, they remain content, even if frustrated, to fantasize without risk. In this sense, they are paralyzed.

Many people respond to conflict in a computer-like manner. A read-out goes something like this:

Tension. Conflict.

Bad.

Isolate it by

1. ignoring it
2. eliminating it
3. subjugating it
4. compromising with it
5. developing alliance against it

Important factor: eliminate tension as soon as possible.

What does this process mean?

First, the process labels all conflict (like pain) as "bad." But like pain, conflict is a signal: it indicates that there is creative work to be done. Negotiations need to take place. If conflict is labeled as "bad" across the board, then growth is hardly possible. There are really three levels of conflict:

Minus	Neutral	Plus
violence	competition	drama
war	bargaining	fun
death	mediation	opportunity
rape	scarcity	adventure

The minus factors are undesirables. But the person who is ready to cope with conflict can turn even these factors into learnings that will be advantageous, too.

A young black matron whose daughter was murdered in a ghetto gangland fracas recently established, with the help of other parents, a citizens' committee to work toward the elimination of the violence and homicides in her community. Her labors seem to be feeble, as she works against great odds. But even if she saves some from the fate her sixteen-year-old daughter met, she will succeed. She is striving to make a tragedy the launching pad of change.

The very word "conflict" implies "to fight together." To have a conflict, there must be, by mutual agreement, an encounter. Any encounter can lead to resolve, reconciliation, and growth. (Growth here implies new learning and new behavior.) In trust, we take the risk that conflict may not lead to good results. High trust — high risk — high productivity. At times, high trust and high risk can mean a cross. This is the risk of the actualized person.

Second, this process implies that the computerized person returns to his built-in "savior" patterns for protection. He wants someone else to deal with the conflict. To ignore conflict is to play the game of blind man's bluff. This is like looking at the green crayon knowingly and calling it red because someone has asked for a red and it seems to be too troublesome to bend over and pick out a red.

Such an approach may be helpful with some harmless snakes and lizards, but it is dangerous with hurricanes, earthquakes, and tornadoes. This approach is also inadequate for social blights, such as welfare abuse, minority oppression, crime, and violence.

One way to eliminate the conflict is to reason about the opposition: "If we can't get along with them, we'll simply vote them out, or get out ourselves." Sometimes, it is said another way: "He can't live forever. He'll die someday. And then. . . ." There is no resolve here. Only displacement.

To subjugate the opposition means to beat down, defeat, tyrannize. This, of course, is a useful and quick method, generally associated with the brutal military processes and the Mafia techniques rather than with civil relationships preferred by a democratic order. Those who live by this rule usually die by this rule. But they readily justify the rule. The ends, after all, justify the means. The consequences are: (1) a two-class system of haves and have-nots; (2) the necessity of remaining strong and in control; and (3) the unwillingness even to listen to another good idea.

To compromise means taking a little of each and not much of anything. This precludes the possibility of resolve and continues the competition in more subtle ways. Someone is always hoping to get everything of importance in the conclusive act. What appears finished is never finished, although an alliance may be formed.

The alliance is literally an unholy affair. Cal and Zeke dislike each other with intensity. But they both dislike Tom more. For a time, they make a pact to work together until Tom is no longer a factor with whom they have to reckon. When the task is over, Cal and Zeke go back to their unresolved squabbles. We have seen this process happen between countries, in business, in politics, among educators, in churches, in social circles, and in families. Husbands and wives, compounding unresolved grievances by daily aggressions, can set these grievances aside for a time to see a child or friend through tremendous periods of illness, grief, or tragedy. But when the first signs of easement come, the old matters reappear and the battle is on.

These computerized reactions tend to develop in one of two neurotic defense patterns: TO FIGHT OR TO TAKE FLIGHT.

Those who remain in between the fight and flight patterns we generally note to be ambivalent. The ambivalent are the immature, the indecisive. They do not dare, nor do they want, to offend anyone. On the other hand, the person who takes flight withdraws, hoping that the "bad" situation will eliminate itself. He is generally one who yields easily to boredom, comfort, and pleasure, is disinterested in unstructured events, is critical of process, feels powerless to affect life, feels fatigue easily, fears being misunderstood, and, in general, expresses a high level of anxiety.

The fighter is more aggressive. He seeks status, often appears cynical, tends to scapegoat by blaming others for his own discomfort, and is often blind in his battle against an uncertain foe. The fighter stands a better chance of creative resolution than the passive person, but he does need to give fuller consideration to his strategies.

What is the actualized person's alternative?

Collate. Integrate. Negotiate.

The most feasible simile of integration is the symphony orchestra. Every person in the symphony is a potential source of conflict. He may play wrong notes. (He could even play the wrong piece.) He may not keep time with the others. His instrument could be out of tune. He may lack the adequate skills. Only when these different and unique individuals ply their skills seriously and IN CONCERT can the proper tension make beautiful music. The violinist's task, for example, is to create the right amount of tension between bow and string at the right time to create the right effect.

Tension (conflict) is essential to all kinds of learning. The action parable helps engender sufficient here-and-now tension to make meaningful learning possible. Those who fear change most fear the media of change. It is easier to control the more abstract suggestion of change than an actual change. But change happens to us all, by deliberate action or by default.

The biblical record is full of illustrative matter. The very early stories of the Hebrew patriarchs, prophets, and seers are stories filled with conflict. The psalmist captures the spirit of it in this song:

> The Lord preserves the simple;
> when I was brought low, he saved me.
> Return, O my soul, to your rest;
> for the Lord has dealt bountifully with you.
> For thou hast delivered my soul from death,
> my eyes from tears,
> my feet from stumbling;
> I walk before the Lord
> in the land of the living.
> I kept my faith, even when I said,
> "I am greatly afflicted."
> (Psalm 116:6-10)

Earlier the psalmist recorded this same spirit of contrition in the midst of conflict when he uttered,

> But when I thought how to understand this,
> it seemed to me a wearisome task,
> until I went into the sanctuary of God;
> then I perceived their end.
> (Psalm 73:16-17)

Learning must be done in the midst of tension. The church, then, must be ready to learn from its sufferings and the world's pain.

This kind of learning will become increasingly the means of church development. The world is full of pain. Not only are there natural causes of pain, but restless and demented persons inflict pain upon others. We also face the divisions and strife which come when dissenters raise their voices in protest against things as they are. The church will take the broken pieces and mend the relationships that have frayed in the hope of building anew God's kingdom. This task is nothing less than that given to Jesus and his disciples: to take all conflict and work with it until it is utilized in the most sensible and creative ways for the benefit of God's mission. This assumption of the creative nature of conflict is the very reality of the whole cross experience.

Conflict is born out of raw human interaction. It is a process in which disagreement, differences between two or more persons (or groups), and antagonisms attempt to drive or restrain each other. This conflict occurs on several levels:

1. Intrapersonal (within myself)
2. Interpersonal (between persons)
3. Intragroup (within the same group)
4. Intergroup (between groups)

In order to find resolution, one party to the conflict must be committed to a win/win position, that is, he must, in his openness, seek to build new understandings. In situations where defenses are high, this approach is never easy. It takes great patience and perseverance. Each person must come to the negotiation assuming full responsibility for himself and willing to assume responsibility for the dynamics of the encounter. Two things can happen: (1) The points of view can be polarized before entering into a long, painful process of arbitration leading to consensus, risking an inflexibility that suggests that each party is "locked in" to his own idea; or (2) The points of view can be put aside, while a "third party" (or the group itself) seeks out as many different alternatives as possible, remaining flexible and uncommitted to one point of view or another during the process. In the second case, the group will develop what data they can amass before the final decisions are made. They will hear all the alternatives. They will strive for consensus. Of necessity, there will be a high degree of mutual respect among the participants. The conflict, whether it be of the first order, polarized, or the second, reasonable, must be dealt with wisely and concluded with some resolution.

As suggested and when necessary, the leadership will use a variety of techniques to help the group look at all sides of the issues in question (i.e., diagnostic tools, fantasy, brainstorming, role reversals, mirroring, multiple role playing, flashbacks, alter ego, and nonverbals).

This way of handling conflict can become more meaningful if the leader will lead a small group, or two small groups, into one or two simulation games. (A simulation game is a structured event that is "like" a real, everyday experience. Learnings can be drawn from these happenings.)

Divide the group in two. Share with them the following plan, and urge them to agree to enter the simulation game with spirit and a determination to win. The object of this first simulation game is to survive a simulated war. There are two sides at war with each other. There is time for considering how they will resolve the animosities. (The longer simulation is carried on, the more intense the feeling becomes. The process should not take longer than two hours and can be done in one half hour.) The alternatives are:

1. If both sides elect to fight, both sides are annihilated.

2. If team A decides to fight and team B decides to negotiate, team B is annihilated.

3. If team A decides to negotiate and team B decides to fight, team A is annihilated.

4. If both teams decide to negotiate, both sides survive.

The rules of the game suggest that each team meet and decide by consensus how they will move toward the other team. At any time either team may send emissaries to the other team to test out their feelings, negotiate, or spy out their intent. They may or may not be received. The process is the responsibility of the teams.

Watch the action. At an appointed time, ask the captains to present their final resolution to the arbitrator (designated leader). Observe the feelings and tensions as the groups come back together. Read the results and begin to examine the feelings.

Ventilate. Identify. Analyze. Generalize.

Enlarge upon those matters which tend to heighten the conflict utilization learnings. Can you note intrapersonal, interpersonal, intergroup, and intragroup tensions? Did the group really play the game? If not, why not? Did anyone discover that the happening could be more real than he had anticipated?

A second simulation is just as meaningful. The directions are simple. The action can take from two to four hours. Ample time should be allowed for rehashing the events, resolving tensions, and to pool learnings. This is called the Red and Green Simulation.

Give each of the participants, who are equally divided into two bodies, a color identification (paper, crepe paper, badge). Give the following directions:

We will be involved for the next _____ hours in a Red and Green Simulation game. You have been arbitrarily divided already as indicated by the colors you hold. Room _____ (the least attractive room) will serve as the Green team's community. Room _____ (the most luxurious room available) will serve as the Red team's community. The Green team will be known as the "have-nots." They work for the people who wear the Red. They have little power of their own, and often find it necessary to turn to the Red team for help.

The Red team are the "haves." They hold the balance of power, select all the community leaders, live in the best homes, and control the city's wealth, jobs, and social benefits.

Stop the instructions and say no more. Just wait. There will be questions. Do not answer them unless they are to clarify the above instructions. Ten or fifteen minutes will be needed to get the simulation in motion. (If nothing happens, what does that say to the group?) More than likely, after the simulation gets moving, it will be hard to break into it to pool learnings. If the experience is to be intensified, two or three other community groups may be added: the news media, the mayor's office, a welfare pressure group, black militants, women's liberation, S.D.S., etc.

When the appointed time arrives, stop the action. Internalize. In small encounter groups, discuss the experience.

Ventilate. Identify. Analyze. Generalize.

Again, the elements of conflict should be identified. Discuss alternatives for resolution. Examine the personal dynamics. Discuss the polarization that occurred. How can we work within a polarized situation? How could we have prevented polarization? How did the participants feel throughout this encounter?

Consider now all the creative factors you have experienced in your life. Do they really come in times of quiet and inactivity? Or have they not come, sometimes by accident, in the midst of, or just after, some struggle? Conflict can be an agent of growth.

What did Jesus mean by the words: "Unless you become as a child . . ."? Jesus was not referring to the intellectual, social, and/ or chronological development of the person, but to the emotional level of a person's life. We learn and teach in concrete ways at all times, even as children do. Our experiences fill our abstractions with meaning. This observation suggests, again, that our visceral considerations are more important than our abstractions in the teaching-learning world. In our sophisticated world of isolation and restraint the visceral aspects of our life have been sublimated. Consequently, our loving is either "detached" or puny. Even sex has become the instrument of lust, separated from our human passions. No wonder we insist on everything remaining smooth. Conflict forces us to deal with our feelings: good, bad, and indifferent. If we prefer to remain detached, apathetic (without feeling), rather than risk our strong passions, we will attempt to neutralize all conflict, making creative learning impossible.

Creative learning and innovation go together. But where have all the innovators gone? There are a few who continue to labor in the world of exploration and discovery. As always, security needs and the need for new adventure are at odds with each other. But they have never been so at odds as they are in our time of intensive and massive change. In all of this, WHAT HAS THE CHURCH GOT TO OFFER, especially to those who are ready for something more than "playing it safe"?

"God did not give us a spirit of timidity," the author of Timothy reminds us, "but a spirit of power and love and self-control" (2 Timothy 1:7). This suggests that there is a certain TOUGHNESS about this love of which we speak, a toughness that will let the most fearful test out life.

An action parable that may help a person realize his own capacity for conflict is known as the *press*. Ask one person who seems to be the most fearful in the group, "Whom do you consider the most difficult to confront in this group?" (If he says, "everyone," then select one of the more formidable persons.) Tell the two persons to meet each other in the middle of the circle. Ask the group to observe what takes place.

To the submissive, say, "Place your two hands on her (his) shoulders. This is known as 'the press.' Press her (him) down to the floor in any way you feel you must in order to get him down on the floor. The only condition is that, once you have him down, YOU MUST ALSO GET HIM UP. Remember, this is to be nonverbal."

To the person being pressed down, say, "You may respond as you feel. You may resist, yield, or whatever you feel you want to do passively. You may not take the offensive. This will also be true once you are down."

Let the action take place for a time. At first, there are feelings of hesitancy. Then, the confronter will make various attempts at getting the person down in steps, physically. He may use force, guile, flirtation, pleading, or whatever he chooses. He must do it all by himself.

When it is over, reverse the roles.

Discuss it. Ventilate. Identify. Analyze. Generalize. Be sure the original confronter ventilates his (her) feelings. This exercise is often done between a frightened man or woman and a strong-willed man or woman. This polarization should not deter the encounter. Trust the process and the group response. Feelings may run high, but that is not the worst thing that can happen.

This whole process, which it might be helpful for the whole group to go through in pairs, is an attempt to deal with aggression and strong aggressive feelings hitherto inhibited because the protagonist felt that the object of his feelings would either fold under the weight of his attack or retaliate and destroy him. In the discussion that follows this structured conflict, he discovers that neither assumption is necessarily correct. People with whom we come in contact daily are tougher than we often assume. They are certainly tough enough to handle what pressures an honest confrontation bring to bear.

The church today has generally robbed its membership of its effectiveness over the past years by emphasizing the importance of "keeping things smooth," being "nice," complementing life by giving the "religious trimmings" of Christmas and Easter, but by not getting too tough or too involved. Why is this toughness so strange to the church, an institution that is committed to follow a tough Jesus? Was he not "tough" with both his friends and his foes? We could learn to face conflict by a willingness to meet tension head on. We could learn to cope.

The leader's role in a conflict utilization encounter is very important. In the initial stages, the group members must feel that he is strong, competent, and personally secure enough to stand in the midst of an aggressive confrontation. Moreover, the climate needs to be an open one, with evident trust, if one is to achieve the goals established for this kind of encounter. Every person must be encouraged to accept his own feelings, hold to his own values, and strengthen those ideas which appear to be most helpful to him. If the variables being tested are limited, so much the better. People find that they can handle one or two disconcerting things, but not a multiple number at the same time.

In conflict utilization, there is a tendency for persons to "get honest." The leader needs to take careful note of those who use the word "honest" as a whip and/or as a shield (hiding place). There is a difference between being "honest" and being "truthful." A person may be honest in his rage in a confrontation. But he may say, "I'm really ready to let you have it for what you just did";

when in fact, this hostility is a defense rather than legitimate anger. His rage may still be toward someone who is taking the brunt of things for the "father" he never had, rather than toward a person in the here and now. This transference needs to be carefully filtered through. Verbalization will often allow this filtering, as it does in a more positive transference experience.

Jesus was a man who met conflict well. He did not seek it out. But when it came, he met it, regardless of the quarter from which it came. He did not "play it safe." Can we do less if we follow him?

12. PLANNING AND DESIGNING

"Would you tell me, please, which way
    I ought to go from here?"
"That depends a good deal on where you
    want to get to," said the Cat.
"I don't much care where — " said Alice.
"Then it doesn't matter which way you go," said the Cat.

Is this not sometimes the condition of the church? In a time of fevered change, where is the church going with its message and its mission? The imperative is to develop a process that will permit the church to be more aware of the conditions that surround it and to gather sufficient information to enhance a disciplined analysis of what those conditions mean so that the church will, in turn, be enabled to develop relevant objectives, establish priorities, cull out useful techniques to do the necessary job, and get on with the action demanded. Relevant action or change is the desirable end of all that takes place in experiential education. In biblical terms, such change is known as a conversion, "being made new." Planning and designing for the new is the exciting task of the trained and skilled churchmen. Human relations skills give a person an edge on immediate events. They help him cope with change. At present, the church is operating without that edge. There has been too great a time-lapse between the discovery of the new and the refinement and utilization of the new, a lapse which forces the contemporary church to address itself continually to yesterday's problems. As churchmen we must move into the unknown with action-research skills which have been developed by a thoroughly sophisticated technology without losing sight of our Christian mission and ministry. Our commission remains the same: "Go, teach." (See Matthew 28:19-20.) But it is set to a new music. It must speak to a new day.

The key to this mission of process is a procedure called STRATEGIC PLANNING. Numerous authors have explained this process at some length.[6] A book related to the process of experiential education should consider this planning process only briefly, to give the general practitioner its essential elements. The general planning skills lead directly into curriculum development, one further essential in the creative process of education for change.

The churchmen tend to claim: "We have good programs; better than the average. But the people fail to respond. They are apathetic and insensitive." More often, it is the program planner who is insensitive.

How often capable professionals in business, government, education, and church can blatantly deny the realities of life around them, even the reality of "instant change" strongly manifested in inflation, technology, and the population explosion! We deny these realities at our own peril, as environmental scientists are disclosing. There must be more planning that will take into account all the factors of reality before us.

The team is the basic instrument in this kind of strategic planning. The rugged individualism, suggested as the virtue of yesterday, is no longer the model for our generation. We will work together, or we will not be allowed to work at all. As a team, we can risk entering the world of severe change as one agent among the many, in the hope that the process of change will be a process in which the essence of the faith we proclaim in Jesus Christ can meet the threats and demands of change and even obsolescence.

Strategic planning provides for two kinds of thinking, vertical and lateral. Vertical thinking is logical and sequential. It is generally precise and follows a step-by-step procedure that is based upon "right" information. Each step along the way is significant. Each step has to be right. This process is useful but cumbersome in the time of high tension and change. In our age, decisions often have to be made before we have enough "right" information.

"Lateral" thinking can be helpful in times of tension. The action parable is an instrument of great value to the lateral thinker. It is the technique which deals with a person's feelings as well as with his thoughts. The imagination is the key to all feeling communication. Fantasy is the language of the imagination. In the action para-

[6] See Richard R. Broholm, *Strategic Planning for Church Organizations* (Valley Forge: Judson Press, 1969).

ble the person is permitted to associate freely, to fantasize, without risking judgment. Failure becomes an integral part of the developmental process, not a barrier to it. Each step is not dependent upon every preceding step. The victory may come "in spite of," or sometimes "because of" a failure.

The strategic planning process uses both routes to its ultimate end of action. The situation dictates the method, though often an interplay between both is more necessary.

The first task is to collect the essential data that is needed to make an adequate analysis of an issue. From the acquired data, a set of assumptions will be developed and tested against new data that follows. The data includes facts, feelings, attitudes, behaviors, projected hopes, current personal skills, and current group skills. At times, this collecting task is lengthy, difficult, and appears cumbersome. But after the initial work, successive action becomes easier as the assumptions are updated and tested against any new data which may become available.

Some basic questions to be answered are:

Who is causing the problem?

Who is affected by the problem?

What kind of problem is it?

The issues can be identified by classifying them in relation to:

Self: conflict about my values, attitudes, lack of skills, inability to express feelings, diversity of perception.

Other: lack of understanding, unwillingness to use all of the resources, lack of skill in conflict utilization, conflict in values, diversity in perception.

Organization: lack of communication (and channels of communication), lack of clarity regarding authority, membership, roles, norms, objectives, power conflicts in decision making, lack of support for innovation.

Society: value conflicts, lack of clarity regarding goals, conflict from other forces, structures.

Then what sources do we need to tap in order to define more clearly the type of problem we are facing? Can we state the problem concisely and clearly in terms of goals which we want to reach?

Collecting data for this kind of definitive work is not easy. It requires careful preparation and collation. The following outline indicates the steps required in this process:

DATA COLLECTION may use any of the following:

Written forms include items, such as questionnaires, scales, essays, projective sentences.

Interviews require skill in asking questions. Avoid "yes" and "no" questions, judgmental and threatening questions, and rhetorical and general questions.

Observation requires training. Take notes.

Memory is the least dependable method. Data should be gathered prior to, during, and after design-skill sessions.

DATA DIAGNOSIS is a process of seeking and using information needed for sound judgment and decision making. It must include:

Expectations, desires: What do we hope will happen? Not happen?

Attitudes: What are our feelings? Motives? Commitments?

Understandings: What do we already know?

Behaviors: What do we feel competent in doing? What skills do we feel that we need?

Experience and abilities: What training have we had before? What other experiences? What skills do we now have?

Responsibilities: What specific job will we do after the training?

Relationships: Do we know each other? Is there trust among the participants?

Pressures: On what basis have we come to these sessions? What did we leave behind? What are our anxieties about what lies ahead?

Situation: How much time is available? Where will the meetings be held? Will the climate be open? Comfortable? Who will develop the design? What resources and equipment will be available? Who is sponsoring this? Who pays the bills? Is there going to be an adequate staff?

DATA ANALYSIS is one of the more demanding steps. Conclusions must be carefully tested against conclusions of others and additional information. A wrong conclusion can lead the planners off on various tangents. The process outline is as follows:

Collation: Drawing together the data (mimeograph, newsprint, etc.).

Trends: What similarities and differences can be noted? What seems to stand out from the data collected? What evidence supports these conclusions (attitudes, behaviors, ideologies)?

Sources: What is the (genetic) source of these concerns? Symptoms? What forces are at work that will help or hinder our movement?

Selectivity: What will need to take priority? What needs to be done most? How do we make the decision?

The process involved in selectivity is not easy. The following model may be helpful:

A. Information from questionnaires indicated skill needs in the following areas:
   1. Need for greater ability to assist with community change.
   2. Need to increase CONSULTING SKILLS.
   3. Need to improve designing skills.
   4. Need to understand the effects of our behavior.

B. The need of the participants to increase their CONSULTING SKILLS seemed important, but the task was too broad for the time available. So CONSULTING SKILLS were subdivided into:
   1. Avoiding producing dependency on the consultant.
   2. Offering helpful resources as a consultant.
   3. Offering DIAGNOSIS of troublesome situations.
   4. The problems involved in entry and re-entry as a consultant.

C. Offering DIAGNOSIS of troublesome situations seemed basic. It was subdivided into:
   1. Identifying the data of trouble when it appears.
   2. Analyzing that data.
   3. Getting the group TO DO ITS OWN DIAGNOSIS.
   4. Avoiding asking judgmental questions.

D. But how does a consultant get a group TO DO ITS OWN DIAGNOSIS?
   1. Using NON-JUDGMENTAL QUESTIONS.
   2. Introducing self-diagnosis instruments.
   3. Recognizing when the group has started its own diagnosis.
   4. Establishing the freedom to look at group behavior.

E. Using NON-JUDGMENTAL QUESTIONS was chosen as a narrow enough, practicable skill. It became the focus from which the purpose of the day-long exercise was drawn.

Consensus: Is everyone "on board" with the decision that is being made?

One very important process that can be used in making an initial analysis of the issues defined as central is known as the Kurt Lewin *force field process.* This is a way of looking at all the forces that interact within the general boundaries of a defined issue; forces that work toward the movement of the present equilibrium in the direction of the desired goal and forces that tend to block that movement, and sustain the current *status quo,* or worse, de-energize the more positive forces, and rob them of their effectiveness.

Take an 8½ x 11″ sheet of paper (or large newsprint) and hold it sideways. (Each team member should have his own paper.) At the top, draw a double line across the paper. Along the left and along the right of the paper, draw vertical lines to meet the horizontal lines, approximately two inches in from the sides. Now, draw a dotted line down the center of your paper. It should look like Diagram A.

DIAGRAM A

ISSUE (problem)			
OPPOSITE TO GOAL	Forces moving TOWARD goal ⟶ ⟶ ⟶ ⟶	Forces moving AWAY FROM goal ⟵ ⟵ ⟵	DESIRED GOAL

Write in the headings but do not put in the arrows. Now you are ready for the force field diagnosis.

In the upper left-hand corner in the horizontal space write: "The problem as I see it is. . . ." Each person should write in what he considers is the prime issue of concern facing either the group or those whom the group represents. Be specific, to the point, and, above all, honest. Consider that issue for a few moments. Is it really an issue? Will it have meaning for the others in the group?

In the right-hand vertical space write, in as specific and measurable terms as possible, "In light of this issue, my goal is. . . ." Can you make it brief; a simple sentence? Is it clear?

In the left-hand vertical space write, clearly and briefly, what appears to be the opposite of that goal. "If we (I) do nothing about this, we (I) will. . . ."

The participant is left with two large empty spaces near the center of the paper. These are the most important sections of the force field process. In the left-hand space, list clearly and concisely those forces that will help the group to attain the defined goal if applied. The participants should put down as many forces as they can think of. In the right-hand side, list those forces that will prevent (block) the group from attaining the goals; that is, those forces which will serve to move them back toward the opposite of the goal. Remember, those preventative forces can be people, groups, budgets, social conditions, etc. They are, more often than not, people. Be open. Be truthful.

After each one has worked on his issue for about twenty minutes, pass the papers around to *all* the others who are present. (The group may need to move around the room to the newsprint hung on the walls.) Ask each person to add to the others' documents all the forces that will enable and/or block them from reaching the goals. This is an important part of the force field process, and it is only helpful if everyone is thoughtful, specific, and candid. When the paper is returned to the owner, he needs to take a colored pencil and mark the forces as follows:

1. — easy to accomplish (E)
   — medium (M)
   — hard to accomplish (H)
2. — not really an issue (NI)
   — an issue (I)
   — a serious issue (SI)

Using the above criteria, note now the first three priority concerns taken from both sides of the forces (enabling and preventative). List them. Each person is now ready to consider the development of clear objectives that will help him cope with those forces that either enhance or prevent the facilitation of his goals. Order the priorities. What must be done first? Second? Third? Ask the team to review all the issues. Are there similarities? Can they be merged? Can the team establish priorities of concern using all of the grist from the force field? This list of priorities, then, needs to be narrowed down through the selective process. Now the team is ready to work on objectives and further plans.

Long-term objectives indicate the overall thrust of concern, the ultimate sense of destiny held by the team. As progress occurs, as times change, as persons change, that destiny may be weighed in the balance, found wanting, and updated. Therefore, it needs to be flexible. But even a flexible sense of destiny helps to set the general course of concern, for all the interim action is measured accordingly. A radical shift in this major objective will create a crisis in the skill competence level and the personal security of those affected by that change.

The short-term objectives are defined as simple, clear, concrete, and measurable behavioral statements that are limited in both scope and time (usually within one year's time, and only a small area of priority).

The following questions are helpful in the development of objectives:

Long-range objectives: Where do we want to go "in the long run"? What do we ultimately want to happen? Is the overall objective flexible?

Short-term objectives: What do we need to do now that will help us move toward our long-range objectives?

1. Is the objective based on the data and our data analysis?
2. Is the objective behavioral (not attitudinal or abstract)? What is the desired action outcome (to practice, to learn, to develop, etc.)?
3. Is the objective specific and measurable? What specific skill is needed that can be measured after training?
4. Is the objective clear and concise? Is it single, simple, and direct?
5. Is the objective attainable? Can we do it in the time that we have, with the people, the leadership, the resources, and the equipment we have available to us?

The *plan of action* is the broad picture that suggests *how* the purpose will be carried out. The plan may come from an instant flash of insight from one person, or it may come only after arduous hours of work in a climate of trust. Procedures that can be used include: brainstorming (the listing of ideas through free association, without discussion), previous experience (what has been done before), written resources (what have others done? what do others suggest?), resource persons (consultants), subgroups (special task groups), fantasy (dreaming, without restriction), and the sorting out of ideas and alternatives. The plan needs to be tested: Will it work? Is it exciting? Would you respond to it?

The planning and action may be happening simultaneously. Action is essential in our generation, even before all the information is complete. Thus, the vertical and the lateral planning procedures complement each other. In technical terms, this combination is what we mean by *action research*. We act now while reflection and feedback serve as our correctives. Improvements are made while we are still in motion.

We are ready now to move on from the overall planning process to the more detailed *procedural process.* What has to happen, to whom, by whom, when, and where, to realize the hoped for objectives? (See the Planning Model at the end of the book.)

Smaller task groups can be trusted to work out the details after the initial strategies and overview have been completed.

The next step is a *dry run,* or a "walk through." This part of the process takes time and should be followed by a careful critique, preferably from a person more objective than the planners. Many ignore this part of the process. But seldom does the seasoned strategist fail to do a "walk through" if for no other reason than to become more familiar with the program sequence. It is an opportunity to test out the sequences, the mode of presentation, the availability and working condition of the equipment, the staff responsibilities, to clarify the intent, and to develop confidence and a "feel" for the process that will permit flexibility in a climate of mutual trust.

Now we are ready for the action. Of course, a good deal has already happened. The strategists have had sufficient feedback to have already become involved in corrective procedures. The action of the strategist is on a continuum where things happen right along. The doing is an integral part of the experience, both to the strategist and the educator. The strategist will spend considerable time weaving the findings of the evaluation into the data collection and analysis process as the effort swings into a new cycle of planning, procedure, and action. The previous action may or may not divert the total or a part of the total direction of the long-range objectives. This review of long-term objectives has to be considered before new short-term objectives are brought into focus.

The educator, after a planned experience, has a built-in learning process essential to the experience itself. The procedure is known as "I-A-G-ing." The letters come from the first letters of the words we have been using continually throughout this book: Identify, Analyze, and Generalize. To "pool learners" means to begin a process that encourages learning from a given experience. The responsibility for the process lies with the teacher-learner and the learners. The experience can be: (1) situational, (2) structured, and/or (3) contrived. (See chapter 2.)

Identify: Look at the experience and ask: What happened? What did I observe taking place? What was involved? What were my feelings? What were the results?

Analyze: Look at the experience in more depth and ask: What caused the result(s) that did occur? Can we identify the forces at work that helped or hindered the group in its working together toward our stated objective?

Generalize: What did we learn from this experience? What would we do again? What would we do differently next time? How can we make sure that we follow through next time?

Practice: Plan another experience that will permit the learner to reinforce his new learnings.

The *evaluation* is the final step in the first cycle of the planning process. The basic question is: Did we achieve our desired goal? The evaluation may utilize a questionnaire, a rating scale, a verbal discussion, a sentence completion, a check list, or an interview. Items to be included are: feelings ("right now, I feel . . ."), understandings ("my significant learnings are . . ."), behavior ("the change in my skill performance is . . ."), process ("our group worked together . . ."), future concerns ("what do we need to do next?"), trainer evaluation ("the leadership could be made more effective by . . ."), and did the design provide for change?

The procedural steps for an evaluation generally include:

1. *Ventilation* — Immediate feelings about the experience.
2. *Purpose* — Was the objective appropriate? Clear? Achievable?
3. *Procedures* — Were they clear? Appropriate to the purpose? Did the group "I-A-G" the experience?
4. *Staff Behavior* — Was the staff helpful? Did they work well together?
5. *Summary* — What was learned that you can use the next time? Or what would you avoid the next time?

Evaluations often tend to be tagged on to a planning process rather than to be included as an integral part of the experience. However, a good evaluation could save a great deal of energy and serve as the key to a heightened sense of movement.

Evaluations should not always be held at the end of an experience and/or learning session. They may come at various intervals, purposefully spaced by the leader (or group) to enhance the feedback process. They may occur "out of the blue" because it has become apparent that group procedures have bogged down, and progress seems to be blocked, or they may be built in at strategic spots.

A word needs to be said about "realism." The tendency of many churchmen to overplan is unhealthy, because to become locked-in to a process is a paralysis of the worst kind. It is far better to limit the scope of concern, develop a narrow plan of action, and move on, rather than to work at the large picture and end up simply by cursing the darkness. This reality orientation keeps us from "playing god" and helps us to accept our human role. Jesus had great difficulty in convincing his own chosen disciples of this need. They would have taken the whole world by storm if Jesus had let them. They found it hard to be content with the healing of a withered arm, the counsel given the Samaritan woman, and the acceptance of Zacchaeus. If our planning simply reflects our personal "hang-ups" and zealous enthusiasm, then we have not properly used the team process of check and balance for some objectivity. Our zeal will soon burn out, for we have developed no priorities. We have built in the possibility of repeated failure because we have refused to be both selective and concrete.

The *lateral process* needs to be clarified more if we are to use it in our planning and designing. It is a process that permits the imagination to play a larger part in the whole area of planning. Let me illustrate:

Art Forms: Using paints, brushes, and large sheets of art paper (or crayons) in color, line, and shapes, have the task group members capture on paper what they see to be the future direction of their work. Get some feeling into what is happening. When fifteen minutes of activity are over, let each person explain what he has done. Let everyone freely associate. Let the experience grow. Have a recorder record the key words and phrases developed during the conversation. When everyone has completed his explanation and free association, post the words and phrases on newsprint. It might be well to divide now into task groups which will focus on one or two of the newsprint sheets. Begin to arrange the grist in some meaningful order. What seem to be the trends? What concerns the group members most? Are there any projected priorities? Have the group come together again to report the findings. The trends may be merged immediately, or they may be turned over to a task group to complete the refinement. From this interaction, the next strategic planning steps can follow.

Fantasy: "Today is _____ (one year from this present day). We are meeting to discuss the experiences of the immediate past that indicate everything is going well. Our plans have come to a successful fruition. People are happy. Progress is made. And above all, we are satisfied with the progress. We are eager to move on to new things. Let's discuss what is happening. Who has done what? How has the group about which you are concerned grown? Changed? Be specific. Be concrete (you can do this in fantasy, you know), the more specific, the better. Describe things as they are in your imagination." Have someone record the key words or phrases that will capture the intent of our imaginations. Let everyone share in building the "big picture" of success. This is the development of vision.

Take a good look at what has been said. Summarize. This picture becomes your general objective. Write it out in behavioral terms: simple, concise, and measurable. Now ask the question, "What needs to happen to us as individuals and as a group if this is going to happen? What skills are needed? What resources are needed?" Let task groups set to work developing strategies and procedures that will enable the group to bring the objective into reality.

Drama: One method that will enable persons to free themselves from the past and stimulate their readiness for experimentation in the immediate is the impromptu drama. Develop small teams of "actors" and suggest that they work together for fifteen minutes thinking through an impromptu scenario that will say for them what they see as: (1) the way the group functions now; (2) the way they would like to see the group function, and/or (3) the anticipated objective behavior that they would consider as a vital kind of behavior for the group in the future. This can be humorous. The idea is to liberate and stimulate the imagination. Following each presentation (or after all of them), freely associate. Be sure a recorder writes down the key words and phrases to help in the recall process following the discussion.

Free Association: This free association may occur in a brainstorming session, or following similes that project anticipated objectives of individuals within the group, or simply as individual fantasy periods (silent time). Encourage the group to bring out all the words and phrases that come to mind, even if they seem irrelevant. The weeding out, the selection, needs to be done later. A recorder is helpful.

These procedures are not substitutes for the hard work of data collecting. But they are often helpful procedures in developing more grist, or in building viable assumptions and exciting visions that need to be tested out later. One of the most important features of this process is that it tends to free us from our past images and experiences. We are so limited by what has happened that everything we plan ends up looking like everything we've done. The imagination needs more stimulation.

Planning and designing curriculum is not a once-and-for-all experience. It is a repetitive process. Taking small, narrow views of an ultimate destiny enables a group to take steps that will eventually lead to the goal, but each step leads only to the next. And each step requires a full evaluation of what has gone on before.

"Learning through encounter" is not easy. It is hard work. It requires continual involvement, personal resilience, deep discipline, and a tremendous willingness to enter worlds of tension that can be just as destructive as constructive, depending upon the person(s), environmental conditions and the process selected. Above all, this kind of learning requires the willingness to risk failure. Change sometimes occurs immediately. In other cases it takes years. Breakthroughs may develop setbacks. Change may be reversed. But that is life. And as long as we have life, it will be that way.

The important thing for us is to move out into action, actually to risk. Then, in the spirit of reflection, we must withdraw long enough to internalize what has happened, analyze the dynamics of the situation, and prepare ourselves for a new encounter. The Gospels picture Jesus following such a pattern of action: encounter experience, then withdrawal to a place of seclusion (the people hunted him down on occasion) where he could consider what had taken place, instruct his inner circle of followers, and lay plans for the next encounter.

Above all, don't quit or "grow weary in your well doing." That, in an age such as ours, is the great temptation of the struggling soul. Hold on! Hold fast! Labor on! "Press on, toward the high calling of Jesus Christ."

PLANNING MODEL

Set aside a full day to meet with the teaching-learning leader team. The following outline may be helpful in designing that day while at the same time modeling the procedure.

Givens: Twelve teacher-learners of the church school leader team will attend a one-day training encounter at the retreat center, Saturday, from 8:30 A.M. — 9:30 P.M. Two meals and two coffee breaks will be provided.

Data: — Ten of the twelve persons have gone through the national curriculum workshops held in the association for two years in a row. There is continuity, concern, and commitment here.

— Two of the participants will be new to this group.

— Five of the twelve are men.

— The pastor will be present as one of the twelve, but will leave early.

— The ages range from twenty-two to sixty-three.

— The church has arranged for child care for the children whose parents are attending.

— There is great enthusiasm for this type of training, since it has relevance to all areas of a person's life.

— There is some antagonism between the seventh and eighth grade leader team and the ninth and tenth grade leader team.

— Three persons have requested the focus for the day to be on planning and designing curriculum. The others, by consent, agreed to it.

— Transportation to the retreat center needs to be arranged.

— John, age sixty-three, in spite of his enthusiasm over the past training and the new curriculum, has had trouble changing his teaching posture. There is resistance in his class to the whole experiential education process. "The old fashioned Bible lesson is good enough. I want to learn about the Bible," they claim. Involvement threatens his class members. Several have quit the class. John is a gentle and genial Christian.

— The eleventh and twelfth grade leader team is experiencing a tremendous response from their young people. They are alive with enthusiasm.

Data Analysis: We will be working with a mixed group of teacher-learners for one day, with the enthusiasm heavily weighted on the more positive side. Two persons will be new and will need to be brought "on board." John will need encouragement. Two leader teams will need time to work out some apparent antagonisms. The senior high leader team may be able to help here. The age range and sex division will strengthen the experience. The pastor will need to consider his leaving early with the group to insure no misunderstandings. There is general acceptance of the day's format, but this needs to be tested out again. The parents who are present should be at ease, since their children are provided for by adult child-care for the whole day in the respective homes. The concern appears to be planning and designing.

Objectives (short-term):

— To increase our awareness of self and others.

— To further develop the sense of teamwork.

— To develop skills in planning and designing experiential education curriculum in the local church setting.

The Plan: — Bring the new members of the leader team "on board" through a team experience that will also increase the team's awareness of their present resources.

— Develop a walk-through experience to familiarize everyone with the planning and designing procedures and terms.

— Divide into two separate simulated "class groups" with the assignment to plan and design experiential education experiences for the other "class group." Consider the live data of the group in designing these experiences.

— Critique and pool learnings from the presentations.

The Procedure:

8:30 A.M. Overview

Present the objectives and develop guidelines for working throughout the day. Make changes as necessary. Seek consensus and commitment. Clarify the schedule and request persons to clarify their commitment. (The pastor should clarify his position, since he must leave early for a preplanned wedding rehearsal.)

9:00 A.M. Experiential action parable related to discovery of resources. Divide into four groups of three, each with newsprint and magic markers. List as many resources on that paper as they can discover from one another. The process will be as follows:

Interviewer: Ask the interviewee, in four minutes, as many questions as necessary in order to discover all his native and developed resources.

Interviewee: Respond to the interviewer by listing all his assets as a resource to this leader team.

Recorder-Observer: Record on the newsprint all the resources under the interviewee's name, while observing the interviewer's techniques. Later, he gives helpful feedback to the interviewer related to his questioning technique (two minutes).

Rotate until all three persons have been interviewed. Time: 20 minutes.

Post the resources. Summarize the total group resources. Develop a master list indicating the variety of resources that may be useful. Time: 20 minutes.

Pool learnings in the subgroups of three and report them out. Time: 20 minutes.

What have you learned about the one you interviewed that is new or important to you? Share it with the leader team in a descriptive way. (This hopefully will bring everyone on board with each other.) Time: 20 minutes.

10:20 A.M. Coffee break.

10:35 A.M. A planning and designing "walk through" with input. Use mimeographed outlines indicating the major points of concern in the development.

Let each subgroup of three pair with another three in collecting data and developing their plan.

Subgroup A (3) plans for subgroup B (3)
Subgroup B (3) plans for subgroup A (3)
Subgroup C (3) plans for subgroup D (3)
Subgroup D (3) plans for subgroup C (3)

It must be clear that this is only a walk through.

12:15 P.M. Free time.

12:30 P.M. Lunch and free time.

2:00 P.M. Complete the "walk through" and clarify at the point of the participants' confusion.

3:00 P.M. Planning and Designing.

Group AB plan a forty-five-minute experience for Group CD.

Group CD plan a forty-five-minute experience for Group AB.

Only twenty minutes of that experience will be administered following a run-through of the planning process used to determine the nature of that experience. The leader will lead a fifteen-minute critique following the experience. Intermittent periods will be encouraged for task and maintenance, observation and feedback.

6:30 P.M. Dinner.

7:00 P.M. Planning and Designing.

7:45 P.M. Presentation #1

8:05 P.M. Critique #1

8:20 P.M. Presentation #2

8:40 P.M. Critique #2

8:55 P.M. I-A-G-ing the Planning and Designing experience. Clarification.

9:15 P.M. Worship and closure beginning with three minutes of silent reflection for each person to think about the persons with whom they spent the day and the task of planning and designing to which they have addressed themselves throughout the day. Nonverbally each thinks of the feelings he has toward others and God. Close with conversation prayer. (Each person speaks to God and the group about how he feels and what his concerns are in a normal conversation tone. Dialogue is possible.)

"God . . . it has been a long but good day. Thanks! I've learned a lot. There's so much more to learn. Help me to live one day at a time, one learning at a time; but always learning. Help me to share my learnings with others; not in words alone, but by the way I live my life every day. I see in Jesus what I'd like to be. I'd like to love as he loved. Help me, God, to discover that kind of power in me and in each one who shares this moment with me here and now. These things I speak because of what I've found from walking with Jesus. Amen."